Great Negotiators

Great Negotiators

How the Most Successful
Business Negotiators
Think and Behave

TOM BEASOR

GOWER

Published by
Gower Publishing Limited
Gower House
Croft Road
Aldershot
Hampshire
GU11 3HR
England

Gower Publishing Company
Suite 420
101 Cherry Street
Burlington
VT 05401-4405
USA

Tom Beasor has asserted his moral right under the Copyright, Designs and Patents Act, 1988, to be
identified as the author of this work.

British Library Cataloguing in Publication Data
Beasor, Tom, 1951–
   Great negotiators : how the most consistently business
   succesful negotiators think and behave
   1.Negotiation in business
   I.Title
   658.4′052

   ISBN-10: 0 566 08728 6
   ISBN-13: 978-0-566-08728-8

Library of Congress Cataloging-in-Publication Data
Beasor, Tom, 1951–
   Great negotiators : how the most consistently successful negotiators think and behave /
   Tom Beasor.
    p. cm.
   ISBN 0-566-08728-6 (alk. paper)
    1. Negotiation in business. I. Title.

   HD58.6.B422 B2006
   658.4′052--dc22

Printed and bound in Great Britain by MPG Books Ltd, Bodmin, Cornwall.

Contents

Introduction

I've written a weekly newsletter, *Negotiation Update*, for over 5 years for a global commercial audience of buyers and sellers. It has contained over 700 tips and ideas on negotiation, buying and selling.

This book is an edited compilation of the negotiation tips and they represent a diary of my own experience as a practising consultant and teacher around the world working with experts in every market sector.

If you'd like to know more about the newsletter then check out my website at www.beasor.com which contains an archive of all the work and an opportunity to subscribe.

I've had the good fortune to meet a wide variety of first-class professionals and I thank them all for the stimulation and guidance they continue to provide me.

1

Practical Hints & Tips

In my years as a consultant I've picked up many tips and handy ideas that I've communicated via my weekly newsletter.

In this first section we have some sensible, simple and practical tips...keep these ideas in your mind and you'll not go far wrong.

Always ask...

This is a short tip but it's very powerful. One of the best pieces of advice that I can offer to any negotiator is this:

"If you don't ask...you won't get."

It can't be more simple. Be ambitious...go for the extra and don't be afraid to ask. Be confident and realise that the other party generally won't offer anything unless you ask for it.

Simple but powerful advice.

Thank and bank

This is the most effective script I have taught and seminar delegates routinely tell me that this one move has generated thousands of dollars of value.

When the other party offers you something, never, never refuse it. Even if it's below your expectations, accept it with the following script:

"Thanks for that offer...it's certainly a step in the right direction and I appreciate your flexibility...but clearly this is a tough deal and we've still got a long way to go before we can get to an agreement. What else can you put on the table?"

It's bad psychology to refuse anything you're offered and just because you've accepted 5% it doesn't mean that you can't then go for 10% and beyond.

Use lightning rods

One of the tactics that I teach in my classes is the use of Third-Party Authority.

This technique allows you to put all the blame on a third party while ensuring that the relationship that you have personally with the other party doesn't suffer.

Here are a few scripts:

"I'd love to pay that price but the bank will only lend me $5000 and you know what banks are like…"
(It's the bank's fault, not mine!)

"I can't get this decision past the suits on the top floor. You know what these executives can be like…"
(I'm on your side and I'm an innocent victim like you.)

"New York will never sign this off…"
(Blame head office…especially if it's a long way away.)

This technique sets up a good lightning conductor to ensure that the blame isn't heaped on you and your relationship doesn't suffer with the other party. You're both innocent victims of a hostile third party.

One word of warning...
Don't pick a person like your boss. First they're easy to identify and could be contacted and second it makes you look junior and powerless.

Own up to failures

I know a negotiator who enjoys using this saying *"Well, we're just have to go in there and fall on our swords in public and see what we can achieve."*

What he means is that when all else fails the best strategy can be brutal honesty...owning up to your failure...throwing yourself on the mercy of the other side.

It can be very disarming if the other side looks you straight in the eyes and says, *"Look, I know we fouled up and there's no excuse for it...we were just incompetent. What can we do to put this right and move on from here?"*

This can be a whole lot better than trying to come up with whingeing excuses and making yourself look anything other than professional.

So the next time you're in trouble try falling on your sword...it might just work.

Slice and dice

My client discovered 17 places in the supplier's cost breakdown where there seemed to be a discrepancy and a need for explanation.

The supplier had offered a very decent package but was not prepared to do battle on every line and with every number.

Suffice it to say that when the negotiation ended the number of slices in the salami was significantly fewer and each slice a whole lot thinner.

This is one of the best buyer's tactics. Asking a seller to justify and explain every line and number is a great way of unpicking their logic. It shows you can be as expert as they are in the subject field.

If you're a seller don't ever think that the buyer won't be looking at the back of the proposal where the numbers are. Be ready for their questions and get your logic ready.

Sellers love package deals. You can hide a great deal of margin inside package deals but they're always vulnerable to a well-trained buyer's slice and dice routine.

Resist the nibblers

One buyer's tactic that I don't much like is the use of the Nibble. A buyer will nibble and nibble so that you make several visits, produce multiple proposals and use up time and energy...and even then they can't commit until just one more meeting.

Badly used tactics damage business deals. Most sellers know when they are being strung along and when a buyer doesn't really have authority and is just wasting their time.

I like to try to ensure that the negotiator with whom I'm dealing has the authority personally. That way you don't have to meet third parties and suffer referrals to committees that waste time and energy.

If you're a buyer then be prepared to drive in a tough deal and make your decision in a timely way. If the answer is "*No*" then just say so and everyone can move on to the next piece of business.

Protracted negotiations are expensive and often counter-productive for both sides.

Present the Russian Front

Here is a quote from Baroness Kennedy in the *Independent* newspaper in the UK on 2 March, 2004. If you didn't really understand what the Russian Front is...well now you'll know.

"The Home Office practice now is to bring forward new legislation which is absolutely abhorrent and totally disgraceful in its abuse of civil liberties and then, when there is uproar, replace it with something only slightly less abhorrent and tell us a a major concession has been made. The concession being made should provide this House with no comfort."

This is a perfect exposition of the Russian Front. If you want to break any bad news start with the worst news. If you want to bring in tough legislation suggest that the legislation will be even tougher and then the voters will be pleased enough with what you originally intended.

Shrewd man, Tony Blair.

Onus Transfer

Recently a client made the following statement:
"Tom, I can only pay 50% of what you proposed as a fee. I just don't have the money but I'd like to use you. What can we do?"

This tactic is known as Onus Transfer. It requires a negotiator to put down their *"Wow"* marker right at the beginning of the negotiation. This is quite obviously a very difficult strategy and breaks many 'rules'.

What is does allow is for both parties to discuss 'how' they can get to the target figure rather than 'if'. Clearly if I had said *"No"* then the tactic would have failed.

What we did in this negotiation was to bring into the deal several key variables that enhanced the value of the deal to me even though the upfront price was so low.

This also shows the importance of having creative variables ready to use so that you don't get hung up on price.

I just hope he was telling the truth!

Building blocks

The subject of the Building Block tactic has come up again recently in a couple of programmes I've run.

If you remember it is a simple process for a buyer to use their volume in small instalments rather than to put it all on the table in one go.

So if you need to buy ten computers...ask for a price for four and negotiate strongly. Then add another four to the deal and negotiate again strongly and then make it ten. This gives you three bites at the deal instead of one.

This can only work if you're a buyer in a negotiated environment. It is very tough if not impossible to do this via a tender process.

If you're a seller then jump the buyer at the first sign of a building block to a high volume level and don't give them a chance to put in the intermediate steps.

It's a very powerful buyer's tactic and should be used regularly.

Call your bluff

Negotiators are often faced with a bluff from the other side. The secret is knowing when it's genuinely true or just a pretence.

"We're looking at a variety of vendors," is just plain buyer conditioning. It's not even worth considering as a bluff. It should be ignored or countered with, *"Well, that's what I'd expect you to do."*

Sellers have been known to say, *"You can have until 3pm to make up your mind but I'm seeing someone else then and they have expressed an interest…"*

Few buyers would give in to that crude use of the Standing Room Only tactic.

The basic principle is that if you reward bad behaviour all you'll get in the future is more bad behaviour. If you yield to a bluff you'll get bluffed every time.

After some experience, I find that I'm almost unbluffable. I'll call your bluff often enough just to keep you honest and to stop you trying in the future.

Remember if you do bluff and it's called then you've got a real problem. Do you continue and try to maintain the bluff or give in and lose credibility?

If you move on a 'final offer' you can never make that statement again, ever.

It's a high risk strategy and one that needs to be thought through carefully.

Give and receive

One of the most frustrating tactics for a negotiator is known as Fading Glory.

In this tactic one party makes a step forward, let's say they make a concession. The other party 'thanks and banks' and then the first party makes a second concession.

The receiving party then 'thanks and banks' again but reiterates that there's still a long way to go.

It seems that despite the move forward of two concessions the 'giver' is just as far away as ever. And they are!

As quickly as the giver moves forward the receiver moves back and the distance remains the same.

Don't let this happen to you. Remember that if you give something you need something else in return. If you merely give concessions you will be perceived as weak and the receiving party will just increase their expectations.

Flinch

Hardly a week goes past without the subject of the flinch coming up on a training programme.

There can be no doubt that good negotiators are great flinchers!

So just in case you had forgotten, a flinch is the reaction that you give to a set of circumstances in order to show surprise or disappointment in order to condition the other party that they will have to move from their position.

"Is that all?" is a flinch reply to an offer. *"I didn't realise it was that bad!"* is the plumber's flinch. *"Sorry, how much?"* is known as the deaf flinch.

What these say is, *"I am expecting more than this so you'd better move!"*

As always with all these tactics it is for you to decide when and if they are appropriate.

Get close and personal

A delegate on a programme this week took my advice and tried to smile a whole lot more and present a more friendly face to the other negotiator.

It was not surprising that the result was many magnitudes better.

It may seem strange that in the battle of commercial negotiation we concentrate so much on the ability to smile and present a friendly face. It really is a key commercial skill.

Far too many negotiators believe that they must have a poker face and be rough, tough characters. This is miles away from the truth.

Good negotiators are people who offer reassurance and help, and who know how important it is for the other party to feel comfortable with them both socially and professionally.

So don't bang your shoe on the table. Smile, get close and personal and then do great business.

Learn their tactics

I must have several documents and training sheets concerning the use of tactics in negotiations. I routinely teach about ten of them...they're the smart moves, the fancy footwork, the gambits of the negotiation process.

Some of them are perfectly legitimate; some are a bit closer to the edge...you choose.

What I want to think about here is the use of antidotes to tactics. By all means develop your own battery of techniques but at the same time ensure that you have a similar battery of antidotes.

There's nothing nicer in a negotiation than spotting a tactic when it's being used. The Russian Front is a great example. The moment that the other party starts using comparisons to illustrate their case we know that the Russian Front is in play.

Learn your tactics...and learn your antidotes...and if you want a list or some extra ideas drop me a line and I'll share them with you.

Know when to draw the line

Negotiators are generally big boys and girls who are more than able to make up their own minds and who do not need a moral nanny.

That's my position when I'm teaching and I then go on to present a whole series of negotiation tactics some of which are wholly legitimate (Salami Slice), some which are a little shady (Third-Party Authority) and some of which can be downright dirty tricks (Colombo Tactic).

Your challenge as a negotiator is to recognise when they are being used on you and have the appropriate response ready.

We all know that dirty tricks are likely to injure the relationship when the other party recognises what has been done to them. The problem is always in trying to draw the line. One negotiator's legitimate tactic is somebody else's dirty trick. One person's authentic behaviour is somebody else's manipulation.

I'm afraid drawing that line will have to be your decision.

Decreasing increments

A subject I teach on each programme is how to space out your concessions.

A concession pattern of 100, 98, 96, 94, 92, 90 is not one likely to be readily accepted by a buyer. Their obvious reaction is that if the seller has come down in equal increments then they'll probably continue to come down in equal increments so the buyer will merely 'thank and bank' and go for more.

A pattern of 100, 97, 95, 94, 93.5, 93.25, 93.1 etc., provides a clear disincentive to the other party to continue asking for more and tells them in no uncertain terms that the shop is shutting soon.

It's a simple principle and one to use every time you need to make a series of planned concessions.

Use real numbers

It's fascinating the appeal that round numbers have to people. The Dow Jones Index has a landmark milestone at 10000 and the £/$ rate is routinely seen as being between 1.5 and 2.0.

Negotiators are often drawn towards large round numbers. They take ownership of a number and for some strange reason won't move from it.

The 10% buyer is a well-known person. For some reason a discount of 10% has far more resonance than 9.5%, and 11% is nothing really great to speak of even though it's more.

There's nothing like a double-digit discount (alliteration!).

Sellers will similarly give away more than they need by going to a large number and offering it as a concession.

Remember…a number like 3.435 is a real number. It looks like it was calculated and has an authenticity about it.

In comparison 5 looks like it was just pulled out of a hat.

Keep your numbers accurate and real.

Don't suffer from round number disease.

Variable variables

This week I was training some sales people from the restaurant business and I asked them what sort of stuff their customers really found valuable when they were clinching the deal.

"Ashtrays!" came the response.

It seems that bar owners place a value on ashtrays, bar towels, coasters, stirrers and so on, way beyond their monetary value.

This is good news if you're a negotiator as you can trade these as variables and get good concessions in return.

Every deal has a large number of variables. Some of them are the key issues: price, volume, payment terms, contract length. Some are, however, definitely less costly to you but they may be perceived as hugely important to the other party.

I've had the same experience in the UK with t-shirts. I've seen wealthy people get very excited over almost valueless t-shirts just because they had an advertising logo on them.

Bargaining can add real value to the deal if you are able to trade cheap variables in return for expensive concessions.

So, always have a bag full of variables when you're negotiating. If you don't you'll end up with nothing else to concede except price and that for a seller is very, very bad news.

Never be conditioned

In the early 1950s there were a series of experiments by psychologists trying to understand behavioural flexibility. They used a fish, a pike, and put it into a large tank of water.

Pike love guppies to eat, so when a few guppies were also put in the tank the pike gobbled them up. Then the scientists put a glass sheet in the tank between the guppies and the pike and time after time the pike bashed into it as it went for the guppies. Eventually the pike learnt not to bash into the glass. It was too painful.

The scientists then lifted the glass from the tank and the pike could now easily attack the guppies...but it had learnt from its previous experience to leave the guppies alone and it knew not even to think of touching them.

The pike starved to death.

Just make sure you're not a pike. Have you been conditioned by your past events never to try to go for a target? Are you a seller conditioned by the buyers not to go for a price rise? Are you a buyer conditioned by the suppliers not to ask for better terms?

Don't be a pike...don't get conditioned...don't starve to death...don't die wondering.

Put down anchors and markers

I teach negotiators not to be the first person to put down a marker. This is invariably good advice and when done skilfully it means that you can gain a real advantage.

I also teach the use of the Onus Transfer tactic and that shows that sometimes you can gain an advantage by putting down the first marker.

Another idea worth pursuing is putting down a marker early in a negotiation in order to show the other party that the parameters of the deal are going to be yours. If, as a buyer, you talk about double-digit reductions then you're saying that 1% or 2% won't do the job. You are anchoring the negotiation in the area that suits you best

As a seller you might like to offer a 2% reduction to show that large discounts are not on your agenda... another anchor.

There are few 'right' answers in a negotiation. You might like to take the tactical advantage by putting down the first marker, or you might think there's more advantage in letting the other side make the first move.

It's your choice.

Set good timing

I've read a few things about using timing in a negotiation to give you an advantage…many of them are dirty tricks and can damage the relationship.

Here are two legitimate issues on timing that have worked for me…they're simple but powerful.

First…when do you negotiate? My body clock is a morning body clock and I'm usually up with the lark. This means that I always want to do my hardest work early in the morning. If you're negotiating with me and I can choose the time then it's an early start…which is good if I'm dealing with owls who get up late and want to do things in the afternoon.

Second…if we're negotiating I want to know when the session finishes. That way I can plan the time and the agenda to suit my priorities.

Never negotiate in a timeless setting. Every negotiation should have a backstop finishing time. That way everyone knows when it's time to go and can plan accordingly.

Two simple things…but in a tough world we need all the help we can get.

Promise rather than threaten

The use of threat is very much a double-edged sword. Used badly it can destroy relationships and can also lead to counter-threat that in itself raises the temperature and can lead to deadlock.

Instead of threatening why not try to do the opposite? Instead of making the other side fearful of the negative consequences, offer them positive consequences if they pursue your line of approach.

Here are a couple of scripts:

"We be more than happy to reward you if you could be flexible on delivery."
instead of:
"If you can't bring forward the delivery time, the deal's off."
(The reward might be quite small.)

"We always offer discounts for prompt payment."
instead of:
"We'll charge you a premium if you pay us late."

The psychology is strong. Reward positive behaviour rather than offer punishments for negative behaviour.

Allow plenty of time

It's pretty well known that when the North Vietnamese government went to Paris to negotiate a settlement, towards the end of the Vietnam war, they scored the first advantage by leasing a property for two years.

In doing this they put down their first marker: they weren't under any time pressure and that they were going to take as long as they needed to get the required deal. Time seemed to be on their side.

The US negotiators immediately understood the power of time pressure in a negotiation.

I find it strange how many times people create disadvantage for themselves by leaving the negotiation of a deal until the last minute so that they're under time pressure. And what's worse is that they often let the other party know.

Plan well ahead and ensure that you have plenty of time. Don't set yourself artificial time deadlines and if you can take more time than the other party can allow then you've an immediate advantage that will give you momentum throughout the whole process.

Irrational prejudice

I teach negotiators the power of emotion as a means of persuading the other party towards your position. In many cases emotion will overcome the power of logical analysis as the ultimate persuader.

Here's the example I always use and it works every time...someone offers you the deal of a lifetime on a Mercedes car with every known luxury and price discount. On any rational analysis this is a great deal until the potential buyer utters the deathly words... *"I've never felt comfortable with a Mercedes...what else do you have? I guess it's just an irrational prejudice with that make of car."*

Suddenly all the specifications, calculations and analysis go out of the window...big style.

We're left with a dumbfounded seller who never believed that their great logical position could be undermined.

Buyer should always keep an 'irrational prejudice' ready for action. It kills 99% of all known logic.

Focus on small numbers

In a previous tip I wrote about the magnetic quality of large round numbers. The obvious example is 10% which for some reason has an almost supernatural attraction to buyers when searching for a discount. I've never yet met a buyer who hasn't asked for a 10% discount or 1 who has ever asked for 11%.

This time I'd like to continue the theme of attractiveness but look at small numbers.

If you say to someone, *"I need five or six dozen..."* the number is imprecise and so are you.

If you say to someone, *"I need exactly 62..."* it's clear you've done some calculations so your number is much more credible.

By the same token decimal places can do wonders for the credibility of numbers. Don't ask for 8% when you can ask for 8.3% which is clearly a much more credible effort at obtaining a discount and the result of some important calculations!!

I heard a story of a company bidding for a franchise and they decided to go in at $10 million. Suddenly one of the team said, *"Hang on…it looks as if we just snatched the number out of the air…"*

"That's because we did!" came the reply.

Eventually they decided to bid $10 million, but this time with the company telephone number at the end.

$10 252 377 just seemed so much better.

They won the contract.

Have the confidence to apologise

When I teach customer service skills and similar subjects I teach people how to apologise.

Many people are reluctant to apologise because they think that it makes them liable and could cause the other party to sue and seek damages. Certainly many car insurance companies don't encourage their policy holders to apologise after an accident just in case it jeopardises their legal position.

If we work in a world where nobody ever wishes to apologise then it's a pretty tough place. Imagine a negotiation where no matter what foul up takes place you want to front it out without an apology to avoid looking weak.

I don't support this position. I like to see plenty of apologies in a negotiation...but with the right script.

"I'm sorry that it happened. There was obviously a misunderstanding..." doesn't affect any issues of blame.

"There's been a problem here and I apologise for that..." Who knows whose fault it was...could have been you, could have been them, could have been an act of God.

Don't be afraid to apologise when necessary. It lubricates the wheels of a negotiation and gets it to roll along smoothly without too much friction and bad feeling. You might find that it actually makes your position stronger not weaker. It also shows a great deal of personal confidence.

Focus on the deal and avoid arguments

When you're trying to do a deal with someone the last thing that you need is an argument. Your main focus is the end product...the handshake...the memo of understanding.

None of this is likely to happen if you've spent the meeting doing nothing but picking holes in the other side and making them feel that you're an adversary rather than a potential ally.

In the heat of battle it's very easy to get carried away and start to see the other side as the 'enemy'. You get locked into positions and issues of pride set in.

Don't argue with the other side. Don't push them away...but pull them towards you in a joint attempt to find a positive mutual settlement.

Now I know how difficult this is if the other side is determined to leverage every last cent out of you and use threats to achieve it. What you've got to realise that by countering threat with threat you may be able to win the argument but the deal at the end of it won't be worth having.

You need to find another strategy than merely hitting back.

Change the team where necessary

I was running a training programme recently and observed a negotiation role play moving along very smoothly in a first meeting.

In the second meeting we had a change of personnel and suddenly the wheels started to come off. The temperature dropped and the relationships noticeably weakened.

This was entirely due to the personal chemistry of the people in the room and something that they had little control over as it sadly deteriorated.

Fortunately there was a third meeting and another change of personnel got the show back on the road. The deal was done and goodwill re-established.

You should not be fearful of changing the personnel in a meeting if the progress of the business is suffering. Some people get on better with other people and rather than try to decide "*Why?*", you may find that a quick team change (or role change) can be effective.

Experienced negotiators are always taking the social temperature of meetings and when it starts to drop they do something about it.

Pause for effect

One of the worst things you can do in a negotiation when you're under pressure is to react quickly without thinking. The other side is putting the argument hard at you and is demanding a reply..."*Well, what do you think? Yes or no?*"

First...let's remember that we don't have to rush. We're in control and we'll do what we want to do and not what they want.

Second, we do three things to give us some space. We can pause and be thoughtful. We might wait a few seconds and then a few seconds more before reacting to give ourselves a little bit of leeway.

Another thing we might do is to use a summary or restatement to put some space in the argument. "*So let's see where we stand...What you're saying is...and what I think you're meaning is...*" This is a stalling tactic that gives us even more thinking room.

Last, we might call for a recess. *"That's a very powerful statement and I need a few minutes to think it through before I can come back to you. Why don't we take a short break and I'll be back in a couple of minutes?"*

People who think before they speak generally do better than those who blurt out the first thing in their minds.

Respond to offers

In the movement stage of a negotiation it often becomes a process of offer and counter-offer.

One side makes a proposal which the other sides needs to rebut and return with a counter-offer.

There is one rule here that should be adhered to. Don't reject offers. If the other party make a proposal to you and you immediately reject it then you're likely to paint them into a corner and force them to wish to justify their position more forcefully.

Nobody likes to be told that their little baby is ugly so when an offer is rejected a certain amount of pride becomes involved: people take rather too much ownership of the positions they've created and lose sight of the value of the done deal.

No matter how poor or unpleasant the other side's proposal you should not reject it out of hand.

How about this script:

"That's an interesting offer, Charlie, I'd like to discuss it with you but I'm not sure I can agree to all of it."

In fact you might not be able to agree to any of it, but we can leave that piece unsaid.

"Christine, thanks for those numbers. You're a tough character and I'm going to have to push you hard here."

In fact I'm going to push all your numbers into the bin, but again we'll leave that bit unsaid.

Let's keep it friendly. Pride is not our friend here when people feel threatened with rejection.

Show ambition

I often use the acronym 'ABC': ambitious but credible.

This time I'll give you some ideas on how to be *incredible* and still survive.

Most of this hinges on your being able to 'sell' the position. First you need a good choice of words. You might like to try: *"Well, I know it's tough but I'm going to have to charge you a premium here of 6%..."* This is good because it allows you to move when you show some feeling for the other side's difficulty.

"I can offer some flexibility but we're going to have to start in the region of 25%..." Implying flexibility allows the other side to come back at you and for you to move while allowing you to set the starting point where you want it.

"I'm an ambitious guy...and I'm not apologising for that so we'll have to look at full list price for this order..." Ambition is never something to apologise for so it's a good means of putting down your marker but allowing some space for movement afterwards.

"I know you'll hate me but I can't offer better than a 1% discount at this stage..." is a use of emotion and the words *"at this stage"* imply possible movement at a later stage.

Be ambitious and try to be credible but always err on the side of ambition if you can.

Know how to haggle

In negotiation jargon we describe a compromise as a splitting of the difference based on one variable. This variable is more often than not the price.

When we have more than one variable we would describe the process as bargaining...the exchanging of variables.

Although we believe that difference splitting is not a powerful behaviour it does have its moments and one of these is when we are haggling over price and nothing else but price.

This is how we'd teach the ancient art of haggling. First you have the other party's position. We'll call them the seller. You then have your target price. You then must put down the first marker.

In simple terms imagine this:

Seller's price – 100.
Buyer's target – 80.
Buyer's first marker? Let's call it 60.

This marker of 60 allows you to move 20 units and the seller can be moved 20 units. A nice equal process towards a deal.

If however your target is 70 then you'd put down your marker at 50 and then you'd have 20 units to move but you'd need to move the seller by 30 units. You'd need to ensure 1.5 units of movement by them for 1 unit of movement by you. This is tougher and needs plenty of thought.

Never haggle without these numbers and targets in your head...almost certainly the other side knows them exactly.

Never accept the first offer

There are very few rules in negotiation…very few right and wrong ways to do things. Most of the time it is a tactical call and you have to make the best sense of the situation at the time.

There is one rule, though, which is close to being an absolute…and that it is never to accept the first offer. It is against the laws of nature for anyone in a negotiation to expect the other party to accept your first position.

You can rest assured that this offer will be 'thanked and banked' and you'll be led towards your second and maybe third offers en route to finding the final position.

When someone does accept a first offer several alarm bells start to sound:

Was my offer too generous? Perhaps I should withdraw it.

Are they desperate? I'll aim for the stars.

What's wrong here? Who are these guys?

These guys are mugs and I'll take them to the cleaners!

None of the above 4 is very pretty and it shows that not only are you accepting a bad deal but you're getting no credit from the other party for doing so. This is real lose/lose negotiating.

Just learn to play the game and remember this simple rule: *"Never accept a first offer."*

Focus on value not price

I recently negotiated a deal where the last thing on my mind as the purchaser was the price.

I knew that I was in a large chain store and that the price was more than likely fixed so I left it and looked elsewhere for value.

I ended up buying a computer with a free case, extra RAM and a deduction on some extra software.

What I was interested in was the total cost of the package…not the price on the tag of the computer.

So…not for the first time in these tips, I'm sure…here's the message to buyers: concentrate on cost not price. For sellers it's about the value of the deal and not the price on the tariff.

AS buyers we'd then talk about the total cost of ownership compared with the acquisition price. As sellers we'd look at the lifetime value of the customer.

The longer the timeline the less emphasis there will always be on the upfront price.

Ask for 11%

On a recent training programme I asked a group of buyers if they'd ever asked for a 10% discount in their negotiation careers.

The answer was a unanimous *"Yes"*.

I then asked if any of them had ever asked for an 11% discount and you can guess the answer.

It's amazing the power of round numbers and the allure of 10% as a number.

Of course, sellers have known this for a long time and have factored it into all of their preparation.

So buyers…don't ask for 10% all the time. By all means get your 10% discount and rejoice but then go for the extra. If you only got just 1% extra every time (11% instead of 10%) just think what your cumulative savings would be at year end.

You'd have much more than enough to send me a Christmas card with a thank you for the tip.

Take credit for a strong position

I'm often asked by clients to help them with live negotiations. This is like going to the doctor: most people do it when it's too late or because all else has failed.

The conversation often goes along these lines: the client is in a desperate position, the other party has all the aces to play and can I help them escape from this weak position?

One of the first activities that I ask any team to perform in this position is to write out two lists: one entitled 'We are strong because...' and the second 'They are weak because...'

It's amazing how this liberates people's thinking.

Ironically you can be sure that the other side also thinks they're in a tough bind and both parties are dreading the event.

Without exception parties in commercial negotiations are in a stronger position than they would give themselves credit for.

Even in monopoly positions there is always a point of leverage, a weakness in the other party that can be exploited.

Don't be a Jonah...things are never as bad as you think.

Control meetings

It is always advantageous to control a negotiation meeting. I'll share with you some of the best methods of achieving this.

The first and maybe best way to control a meeting is to ask lots of questions. When you ask good, searching, open questions you force the other party to think in answering your question. This puts them on the spot and allows you to relax while you frame the next question.

People often think that telling is controlling. It isn't. When you find a great talker it merely allows the other party to switch off and places them under no pressure at all. Keep them thinking and answering...that's the best advice.

The second effective controller is to summarise regularly. You should always ensure that it is your party that does the summary. First it places you in control and second it stops the other party from having a selective memory and forgetting key issues.

Last, there is interruption. If you wish to interrupt somebody don't hesitate to do so. Reach across the table with your arm out and say: *"Richard, can I just interrupt you a moment. I've a question I'd like to ask before I forget..."*

It always works. Use their name and the behaviour label *"Can I just interrupt you...."* and they'll never find you to be rude.

If they fight back assertively ensure that you do interrupt.

These 3 techniques will always give you a firm advantage in controlling the meeting.

Understand pride

People are emotional characters and they bring a ragbag of their emotions to the negotiation table.

The emotion that I fear the most in a negotiation is PRIDE. If this is then mixed with testosterone we have a very explosive mix which can hijack a sensible negotiation badly.

When people invest too much personal pride into a negotiation they very quickly dig themselves into trenches and start to throw bombs at the other party.

They become reluctant to move or deal because they feel that they will lose face if they are seen to be weak. They start to defend their positions irrespective of their merit and often start to deny the need to do a deal because their pride will not allow them to be seen as weak or to be seen to lose.

Effective negotiators understand pride. They know that the other side is bound to be proud of their position and will have invested a great deal of feeling into their arguments.

Accordingly, successful negotiators do not belittle the other party nor seek to denigrate their argument or them personally.

Most negotiators really want to do a deal. We need to ensure that their pride does not get in the way and we need to encourage them to take up difficult positions by showing awareness, flexibility and encouragement.

Ask for more

All professionals have a vested interest in making a subject look hard and complex.

This is not really the case with negotiation. I believe that essentially negotiation is a simple process and shouldn't be over-complicated.

I say on training programmes that more money is left on tables in negotiations by lack of ambition than lack of skill and I have real evidence for this.

So...starting from now you can be more successful in your negotiations...not by being tricky and using great tactics but by just asking for what you want and then asking for some more.

It's all about confidence. The greatest negotiators in the world will fail unless they have the confidence to see their plan through.

When in doubt just ask. Don't die wondering. All they can say is *"No"* (and that never hurt, did it?).

Keep it reasonable

The Godfather certainly knew how to negotiate. Here's his philosophy:

"Never get angry. Never make a threat. Reason with people."

I've met a few buyers who could have done with this advice. Their first port of call in negotiation was threats and when that was exhausted they tried some more.

Good negotiators are almost unthreatenable. If someone tells me, *"Take it or leave it..."* I'd be almost certain to leave it. No matter how much I want something the rule has to be that if you give in to a threat once you'll just be setting yourself up for more grief in the future. If you don't believe me just ask any parent who's had to deal with their kids recently.

Don't use crude threat. It spoils relationships and overall with professionals doesn't much work. Keep it veiled...and learn some good scripts that don't sound like you're extorting money.

Let's be reasonable out there!

Make it personal

Don Vito Corleone told his family, *"Keep your friends close but your enemies closer."*

He understood well the need to know your adversary and to have a relationship with them no matter how competitive or hostile it might be.

You cannot really negotiate with strangers so ensure that when you prepare for a particularly tough negotiation you do your best to find out with whom you'll be negotiating personally. Ensure that you do your best to get to know them and try to build some arena of a relationship prior to the event.

The more difficult the circumstances the more important it is to get to know people personally.

Politicians understand the power of a 'walk in the woods' where the top people talk person to person and try to create a positive aura.

If you can make your negotiations more personal you'll be moving forward significantly.

Avoid maximums and minimums

One of the most frustrating issues in managing sales staff is when you set your team maximum acceptable discounts.

"You can give away 8% but no more," are the often-heard words of a sales manager.

Off into the field go the sellers armed with their maximum of 8% merrily giving 8% to every buyer they meet. That 8% was meant to be the maximum discount but very soon this maximum has become the minimum as every buyer now receives it.

One of the problems of setting yourself a maximum acceptable level of concession is that it is very easy to jump straight to that level in one go.

You must get there slowly. If a buyer has a maximum contract length of five years to offer they should try to see what sort of deal a three-year contract can gain first.

Making the maximum your minimum is a lazy way of not bottoming out the possibilities in a deal and accepting the path of least resistance. Don't let it happen to you.

Show flexibility on the best price

I often hear buyers asking sellers what is the best price that they can offer for a particular product or service.

It seems that buyers have great faith in the ability to find the 'best price'. It must be the holy grail for purchasers. Hidden somewhere in the deal is a mythical 'best price' just waiting to be discovered.

Buyers, take my advice: don't even bother, it's a waste of time.

The 'best price' in a deal changes more quickly that the Melbourne weather.

If a manager asks me what my 'best price' is for a training programme, I need to ask how many programmes they have in mind, what sort of programmes they are, what the payment terms are, what issues there are with travel and accommodation, what will happen with the training materials, whether development work will be needed etc. etc.

In every one of these cases there will be a range of 'best price' options. Each one will last approximately 10 seconds until we change the terms and conditions of the deal whereupon another range of 'best prices' will emerge.

By all means look for a best price in a deal but don't be too disappointed if you don't find it very often!!

Use allies

I generally keep well away from political negotiations. I much prefer the smell of money when I'm negotiating.

There is one technique that commercial negotiators can learn from their colleagues and that's the use of third-party influence.

Very rarely does any political negotiation involve just two parties. There will be the media, government, other political parties, non-governmental organisations, public opinion and many more. All these agencies can influence the outcome.

Think the next time you're cutting a commercial deal whether there's any way that you can use an ally to exert influence on your behalf.

A judicious press leak could be all you need to persuade the other party to agree. A telephone call to an interested party might give you some extra leverage.

Don't see deals in a vacuum. Look at the context and the environment and see how you might be able to use them to your advantage.

Think in absolute terms

I've often said that I think large organisations are vulnerable because they have so many noughts after their numbers that they tend to disregard 'small' sums.

I hear people saying, *"It's only a quarter of a mill., so it doesn't really matter."*

Well, in my life £250000 is a very large sum of money and while you may think it's trivial I certainly don't.

You've got to think of money in absolute terms rather than relative terms.

Relatively, a quarter of a million dollars might not be much compared with a billion-dollar investment.

But in absolute terms a quarter of a million is a huge sum of money.

Negotiate as if the money were yours. Don't ever disdain a sum of money because it is only 'small'.

All money is real, even if it doesn't belong to you.

If you're not sure about this then ask me to quote for some training on the matter and I'll soon cure you of your complacency!

Fire both barrels

When you're faced with the enemy across the other side of the table it's often necessary to fire off the occasional barrel of shot with a quick refusal of an offer of the need to get an improvement on a first position.

You'll hear yourself saying, *"Thank you for that offer, but I'm afraid you're going to have to do better than that,"* or *"Thank you, it's a step forward but I'm going to have to push you here. It's important to me..."*

These are both correct but remember that they won't be a surprise. A well-prepared negotiator will have a fall back position available and they probably didn't expect you to accept the first offer anyway.

What you need to learn now is that when it comes to the second offer it's now time to fire the second barrel and get that one off the table as well.

"Well, thank you for that revised offer. I think we're getting somewhere now and we may be close to an agreement if only..."

Don't accept the second offer. Fire the second barrel and then get to the third offer. That's where you really want to start from.

Have the confidence to get the movement and remember to fire both barrels.

Hurry slowly

Negotiations can be pretty exciting affairs. There's money on the table, risk to be managed and a crowd of people trying their best to achieve a tough result.

It's no wonder, then, that when people begin the process they go too quickly and make a rather premature start.

Negotiation takes place between people so when you're in the room get to know them. Spend some time in being polite and loosening the tension.

I teach people to be friends rather than enemies and remember it's a double benefit. The more you find out the better (information can be power) and at the same time you'll find that people start to relax and feel that you're maybe someone that they'll be able to do business with.

Don't rush straight into the business agenda. Spend time on the social side and break the ice. That's the opening phase of the negotiation and only when it's properly completed should you think about moving on.

Go for the *'Wow!!'*

One of the most important things that I teach on my training programmes is the need for ambition and a good 'Wow!!'

'Wow!!' is the word I use to describe the best possible thing that could happen in the negotiation. It is your best hope if everything goes well. It's what you're going to aim for and only when you don't get it will you start to accept a second-best fall-back position.

I've said before that negotiators are generally pretty unhappy people. Here's why...they went for the 'Wow!!' and didn't get it so they're having to settle for second best. Alternatively they got their 'Wow!!' and then have second thoughts about whether it was stretching enough and whether they could have got more. Pretty sad people, really.

Ambition and no skill will probably do just as well as no ambition and lots of skill.

Set your targets...good, stretching targets...build in realistic intermediate positions and then go for it with a good, persuasive, well-structured argument.

How could you possibly fail?

Keep going to the end

There's nobody so unsuccessful as a happy negotiator. You'll notice that I used the word 'unsuccessful'. I believe that most happy negotiators are people who have generally accepted second best and have walked away believing that they have a good deal but have generally left a large amount behind on the negotiating table.

Effective negotiators are always pushing at the boundaries, fighting the status quo and in many cases they are unsuccessful and by definition disappointed.

If you're a buyer you get a 5% discount so you go for more. You then get 10% so you go for more. You then try for 12% and then you fail.

Ironically most commercial negotiations end like this in failure. They really must do because eventually the other party will say "*No*" and you'll have to accept it.

Just keep going…ask for more…bank it…go for more… bank it…and then stop when you have to.

Is that success or failure?

Beware email negotiations

I've been asked recently about online negotiations.

The first thing we need to understand is the difference between an online auction and a negotiation.

An auction is merely the placing of competitive bids against other bidders in a controlled online environment. This is most definitely not a negotiation.

A true online negotiation differs from the traditional face-to-face negotiation only in as much as the method of communication is different.

Negotiating by email needs to be more thoughtful and the script needs to be analysed and revised carefully. The meaning of words can be very easily changed by being read in a tone of voice very different from that of the sender.

The use of emoticons tries to offer some tone guides that will be helpful to the reader.

There is no real alternative to a face to face meeting but if you must communicate by email be careful of the words and revise your text most carefully.

Accept and amend

At some stage in a negotiation an offer is put on the table.

At that moment the receiving party has to react. An obvious reaction is to reject the offer and offer an alternative.

I believe that this is half right. Certainly you should have an alternative ready to put forward but it is important to remember how best to do this.

The script should go:

"That's a very interesting offer and it certainly has real merit. I wonder if we could think about it for a moment and come back with a reaction."

"We've given it some thought and what we'd like to offer is a slightly amended version…"

The McEnroe response, *"You cannot be serious…"* only causes deadlock and creates bad feelings.

Accept offers warmly and then amend them slightly. Of course 'amending slightly' often means ripping them up and starting again but done sensitively it shouldn't become a major issue.

Never argue with an idiot

Good negotiators are good persuaders and that means being able to put your case to a variety of people in a solid acceptable format.

I was recently given the following advice:

"Never argue with an idiot. They drag you down to their level, then beat you with experience."

This is clearly true so take the advice and don't argue with an idiot but seek to be persuasive and get your point across.

Remember if communication fails it's usually the fault of the sender and not the receiver. If you want someone to understand your point of view take the trouble to structure your argument so that they be properly convinced.

If you're dealing with the dull and the daft see it as your challenge...

Adapt to an online environment

Successful negotiators are always good communicators. They should be able to adapt to the online world easily.

Here are a few tips that will help:

Make plenty of simple offers and offer flexibility.

Invite suggestions and encourage exploration.

Share information where possible.

Don't overload the message with too much detail.

Don't make accusations.

Don't label the other party's ideas in a derogatory manner.

Don't overreact and start a flame war.

Engage the other party personally.

Always offer some social connections (talk about the weather, sport or something you have in common).

Make it hard for the other party to say *"no"*.

Be nice, but very firm.

There's nothing here that you wouldn't offer as advice in a traditional negotiation but style and form are even more important online and become key considerations.

Prepare, practise hard and have a winning game plan

The people who get the best results in negotiation are not necessarily the best negotiators.

The most successful operators are those who can 'do' their best and not those who 'are' best.

In any game the winner is the person who can take their best game to the pitch that day and put it into action. That's why so many international players often lose. Tiger Woods' best game is the best in the world of golf but he doesn't always take it to the course and can't win every game.

What good negotiators know is that if they are well prepared and do their very best to take their 'A' game into the negotiation room then their success rate will be high.

Nobody has a right to succeed and if you're under prepared and out of practice you'll do badly.

The next time you negotiate be prepared, practise hard and have a winning game plan. You'll do well even if the other side may initially seem to have the advantage.

Remain credible

The use of markers always represents a difficult issue in a negotiation.

On a starter course we teach you not to put down markers until you have to. On more advanced programmes we teach how to put markers down more skilfully.

The easiest way to remember how to do this is to use the principle of the radius of credibility.

A marker should be put down far enough away to be stretching for the other party and it should represent your most ambitious target.

If you put it down too far away you'll look as if you don't understand the market and are unprofessional. Your marker will lack credibility and that may even reflect on you personally.

So, be ambitious, go for the 'Wow!!' but don't get carried away and ask for the moon (and the stars and sun!).

Show style

I spend a great deal of my time talking about skills improvement and knowledge transfer but I'm also finding I spend more and more time talking about acting.

Many negotiators, especially new entrants to the dark art, find that the real barrier to their achieving optimum performance is not knowledge or skill but confidence.

The antidote to this lack of confidence is easy. I tell people to step outside of themselves and just for a few moments be 'somebody else'.

If people can convince themselves to try asking or refusing in this way they'll very soon find that they can easily do this naturally.

Effective negotiators are good actors. They have confidence and know when to use some extra 'style' to get the point across.

It doesn't have to be Shakespeare so give it a try.

Know the opening lines by heart

Whenever I run a negotiation simulation in the classroom or ask delegates to participate in a role play I always force delegates to tell me the exact words that they would say. I want to know the script and I want the delegates to be confident that when they are facing the other party across the table they'll have a confident and persuasive argument ready to put.

This means that if you want to be effective you have to rehearse your lines. You need to ensure that when you're put on the spot in a difficult situation you're not short of something powerful to say.

What this means is practice. You need to practise your opening statements especially and you want to make sure that your ideas are well organised and that you can put them over with real power.

Negotiators are good actors and they certainly know their lines!

Look to the long term

I would say that any fool can do a single negotiation and run for the door.

If you're buying a car or an apartment and you'll never see the other party again negotiation is generally a breeze. You can use the Vice and the Oliver Twist tactics by just keep asking for more and squeezing and squeezing.

Most professional negotiators don't operate in this way. They have to live with the relationship that they create in the first negotiation and it may be that the deal may last over several years and have enormous business and personal ramifications.

On training programmes I tell people that you can only negotiate with somebody once. After that you're managing a relationship and all the baggage from previous meetings is brought to every session.

So, if you're a successful tactical negotiator move up a gear and try to look at the long-term relationship issues. That's where the real payback in big deals is to be found.

Take a break

I've seen many examples recently of negotiations where the ability to take a recess proved very helpful.

I teach the importance of the well-timed recess. There is no doubt that if you are under pressure or merely need time to talk in private with your team then taking the recess opportunity will be useful.

It provides the thinking and breathing space to regroup but more importantly it tells the other side that you are confident and clearly in charge of the process.

So...don't be forced by the other party to react under pressure. Ask for a time out, go into the recess room and get it organised before returning into the main room.

Scripts such as: *"That's an important issue. Give us a few minutes next door and we'll happily respond,"* or *"Why don't we take a short break at this point? We need to crunch a few numbers in order to check our facts."*

Both of these will work well and enhance your professional reputation.

Avoid deadlock

You should always prepare your facts before a negotiation. You can always rest assured that the professional on the other side of the table will have done likewise.

Therefore when it comes down to stating the case both parties are likely to have well-regulated proofs for their points...even if they are opposite and contradictory.

Deadlock will soon ensue if both parties insist that their version of the truth is the ultimate and definitive.

A much better way out of the situation is to use a couple of scripts that will not create too much heat. You can try: *"That's certainly a good point and it's well argued. What I'd say is that you might be able to improve your point by adding..."* or *"I'm not sure that I see things quite the same way. Let me put my version over to you by way of seeking a clarification..."*

Neither of these is perfect. Find your own scripts that work and remember not to drive yourself into deadlock with words like, *"You're wrong!"*

Show discretion

Good negotiators should never tell lies. Lies destroy relationships and ruin deals.

Any deal founded on a lie is always prone to being nullified if the other party finds out.

It should, however, be just as obvious that telling the truth is not always the best policy. It can be ruinously naïve.

This means is that if you are asked a tough question you are under no obligation to answer it.

Buyers asked their budgets can reply, "*We have enough to meet our needs.*" If pressed they can say that the actual sum is obviously confidential.

Sellers asked for cost breakdowns can provide categories such as 'profits and fixed costs' that while true will not always be easy to unravel.

Being discreet is always to be recommended.

Markers

I tried to buy something recently and the seller wouldn't give me a tariff or price list.

They said that they didn't provide one in order to be flexible and able to respond to the marketplace!

This is, of course, a pack of lies. They are desperately trying to stop me benchmarking them against the opposition and the words, *"This quote is good for this telephone call only"* is not likely to make me feel that the deal is being pursued in good faith.

Be reluctant to put down a marker but if you refuse absolutely and then offer something like a 'take it now or leave it' quote you'll damage the relationship.

Markers must be placed carefully on the radius of credibility and with the other party's reaction in mind.

Check, check and check again

The easiest answer to any question is *"No"*. When a person has doubts and they do not wish to commit themselves they'll say *"No"* even when they might be interested. It's a defence mechanism against being railroaded or manipulated.

Good negotiators know that if they go too fast or try to get an early settlement the usual response will be a negative.

The two learning points are: don't hurry the other party and always check again. I like to hear *"No"* three times before I'm sure it doesn't mean *"Maybe"*.

The joys of software

If you want to support your arguments or undermine the opposition, take a laptop computer into the room and ask for a couple of minutes to run the proposal through the machine.

You can then tell the other party that the computer has rejected their arguments and you cannot change the parameters.

Remember, do not be impressed with computer printouts, statistics or thick documents. They can all be easily manipulated.

Stick to the rules

Most people are law-abiding citizens and will follow all manner of rules, laws and regulations if they believe them to be genuine, especially if they're written on expensive paper.

This is the power of legitimacy. It is key in negotiation. If it looks as if it is genuine then often your 'rule' or 'law' will not be questioned.

You could try, "*We won't be accepting price rises next year. The board won't let us. Here's their press release.*" If you're a seller try, "*Here's our new price list freshly printed. It's only a small rise, I'm pleased to say.*"

Accentuate the positive

The more that I see negotiations taking place the more I see closed questions costing negotiators big money. Every time you ask a closed question you are giving the other party the chance to say *"No"*. And they will say *"No"* with great enthusiasm to every suggestion that you have for an improvement to your position.

Remember the script is, *"How can you help me?"* (the open format) rather than, *"Can you help me?"*

Always have the assumption of and structure for a positive response.

Check for real decision makers

Negotiators should know that the people sitting on the other side of the table have the authority to commit to the deal. You may find that you have been wasting your time dealing with someone too junior to clinch the deal and who will have to refer it back to their boss who is bound to ask for another concession.

Check that you are dealing with the real decision makers and if you are not then get every part of the deal agreed step by step before you continue committing yourself without knowing the possible outcomes.

The last thing that you want is for a more senior person suddenly to arrive who wishes to renegotiate the whole deal again.

Enjoy waiting

One technique taught on every course and nearly top of every list of tips is making sure that you don't put down a marker first, especially in low-value deals.

This also includes 'indicative forecasts' and 'ball park figures' which have a nasty habit of being forgotten when they are too tight but of being nailed down as a commitment by the other party when they are too generous.

So don't make a first bid or offer. Let the other party put down their first offer before you commit yourself. Putting down a marker can only limit your horizons and create problems for yourself. If the other party puts down a marker first you may be pleasantly surprised at what you see.

Don't be too eager, it's worth the wait!

Have a healthy disrespect for first offers

If putting down a marker is a potential weakness then when a marker does go down you can rest assured that the negotiator has given themselves plenty of negotiating room below (for sellers) or above (for buyers).

You must learn to have a healthy disrespect for the first offer. It is only the price the other side think you will be silly enough to put up with.

Never accept a first offer. It wasn't intended that you should and you can be pretty suspicious about the second as well. It's when the third offer goes down that prices start to get serious.

Avoid conditioning

Do people lie? Can you believe everything you're told? Let's see:

"We've got several other bids lower than yours."

"There's only one left in stock, so be quick."

"You've only got 5000 bedroom nights to place. I thought you were telling me you were a big customer."

What you see here is the power of conditioning. The ability to convince the other party that they're sure to fail even before they've started.

There is a moral issue about whether these are 'lies' or exaggerations but in either case you should take the comments with a pinch of salt.

Don't let it happen to you. Convince yourself of your power, desirability and success and then condition them about how lucky they are to have your business.

2

Planning & Preparation

Good negotiators are always well prepared. I've always
emphasised this in my tips.

Here is some of the most powerful advice that I've given
to make sure people are well prepared.

Review

At the end of a negotiation it's always tempting to leave and move on quickly. When I'm with a team I try to get them to spend a few minutes looking at the day and trying to manage a decent review.

There are two areas of review.

The first area is the Outcome. This asks if the results of the day were acceptable and were in line with what the team had in mind and whether the parties back at base will find the numbers acceptable.

The second area is the Process. This asks if the way we structured the meeting was right, whether our planning and organising of the whole event was successful. It looks at behaviour…whether we did well as a team and how well we compared with the other side.

There's a long list of items to discuss. Always try to find some time at the end of an negotiation for review. It'll make you better for the next time. Good teams generally learn more from their failures than they do from their successes. I believe that if you can pledge to be better tomorrow you'll be on an upward path to success.

The next time you and your team meet to negotiate ensure that you don't leave the room until you've spent a decent amount of time analysing and evaluating the event and most importantly working out how you can do better next time.

Get the team roles right

I'm not a great fan of large team negotiations…they are unwieldy and need hours of preparation.

If, however, you do find yourself in a situation where a team is required here's a formula for working out roles:

1. You need a boss/decision maker who represents the side.

2. You need a lead negotiator who will drive through the deal.

3. You need technical experts who'll have the knowledge you require.

4. You'll have a scribe who'll make thorough notes.

5. You'll have a coach and process expert who'll ensure you're on the right track.

6. You'll have a junior gofer who'll do the bag carrying.

Get the roles right and you've got a much better chance of succeeding.

Learn the lines

I like to ask my delegates on training programmes to tell me exactly what they'd say to the other party in a particular situation.

I say to them, *"Give me the script…"*

I like to know that when it comes to a tight situation people will be able to use a nice turn of phrase to give them some advantage. It helps when you've got a stock of good sentences that you can use when you need them.

This can't happen by chance. You've got to run these situations through your mind many times and rehearse the situation (either in your head or with other people).

One of the advantages of being older rather than younger is that you've often been in the same situation before and you know what to do. Even if you're at the beginning of your negotiation career you can still benefit if you've managed to learn some nice expressions which you know will always get you out of trouble and give you a step up in the deal making.

Look for the value

So how much is a $10 note worth...?

$10 maybe, but if you're a millionaire, you might choose to light your cigars with a $10 bill. If you're on the poverty line, $10 is what feeds your family.

$10 has a common and certain value. Its value is clear to see and calculate. Its worth to the other party is not quite to easy to calculate. That's uncertain.

This is what goes through a negotiator's mind when they're preparing for a deal. We list all the variables and we know how much their certain value is. AS an example prompt payment has a value depending on time and interest rates. That's the certain value. But money could be less important to a large corporate who are cash rich and much, much more important to a small organisation with a large credit ledger, overdraft and cash flow issues.

Never assume that the other party values variables in the deal as you do. Try to find areas where they're likely to find great value in something that costs you little. That way you're going to be able to trade something that costs you next to nothing and get something important in return.

Test the water

There must have been a lot of old Chinese people around to keep writing all these proverbs but I came across this one recently:

"When you want to test the depth of a stream, don't use both feet."

Now this one seems to make sense to a negotiator. Things never do seem exactly as they are and you'd be a pretty foolish person to expect the stream to be as deep as you might first believe.

I have numerous examples of situations where negotiators were taken by surprise because they assumed the depth of the situation and reality caught them out.

Good negotiators are never surprised. They work things out in advance and do their contingency planning very thoroughly. I hope that's what you do.

Cover the bases

I think that contingency planning is one of the most important pieces of preparation that a negotiator can perform prior to the event.

My delegates have often heard me state that if you're surprised in a negotiation then it's your fault because you should have predicted it.

One way of predicting it more formally is to draw a decision tree; that way you'll have every possibility covered.

Let's look at an example...

You're in a negotiation as a workplace representative for your team. You're trying to work out how the negotiation with the management is likely to go.

You're going to ask for 6% more money...so, what if they refuse...what are you going to do? If you threaten sanctions what are they? If the boss says *"Fine"* then when will the sanctions begin? What if the boss makes a counter-offer? What's your reaction to 3%? 4%? etc?

What if the boss threatens to fire the strikers? And it goes on.

Some of these contingencies may seem far fetched but it's just as well to have covered your bases before the negotiation rather than be caught unprepared in the meeting.

Look at risk, opportunity cost and value

I've started being more demanding in my seminars and have been more stringent in getting delegates to generate lists of variables so that they can trade their way into a winning position and stop being so price focused.

I hope this sounds familiar to many past students.

What I want to add here is the need not only to generate the variable but to put a realistic price tag on it. Example...if you're in manufacturing and you gain an increase in the warranty from 3 years to 5 years then you've gained an advantage...but how much advantage? If you don't know that answer then how can you try to trade it profitably in return for a quid pro quo variable from the other side?

Issues like payment terms are easy – everyone can calculate the price of money – but the softer, less easily calculable variables can often add more value than the hard price-driven variables like volume and contract length.

Look at risk, opportunity cost and value. This type of analysis will allow you to be even better prepared before you go into the room and will allow you to be able to keep a better running score of benefits received and concessions given.

Plan their numbers

Everybody knows that it's important for a negotiation to have parameters. At one end they represent a great 'Wow' result and a 'walk away' at the other.

There is also the same set of parameters for each variable in the deal.

What I'd like to add to this is the need to try to predict what the same set of numbers looks like for the other party. If you can predict the places where the deal is likely to centre then you'll have a clear idea of the zone on either side and can plan the numbers accordingly.

It is much to your advantage to have the centre of the deal in your sights and be prepared for it. It would be a waste of time to prepare for a deal that looked attractive to you only to find that the other party disqualified this and took you to places that you hadn't prepared for.

Plan your numbers and then try to plan theirs.

Use influential friends

Some negotiators are monoliths...single parties reporting to nobody and with no outside influences... lone wolves almost.

These people are actually quite rare as most negotiators do not exist in isolation and have reporting structures, management teams and stakeholders all of whom are likely to have some interest in the outcome.

In the preparation for a negotiation it's often worth spending quite some time working through the areas of third-party influence on the other side and then seeing how far this can be used to advantage.

It may be that you have people on your side whom you can use to add leverage to your position. Your senior people may be able to influence their senior people before, during and after the negotiation process.

This is most often seen in industrial relations and political negotiations where constituencies such as the media and voters become almost as important as the party on the other side of the table.

Play devil's advocate

One of the best ways to prepare for a negotiation is for you or your team to spend a lot time thinking about what you'd do if you were in the other party's shoes.

You might like to appoint one of your team to act as devil's advocate and ensure that whatever your case, argument, facts or evidence you test its validity and robustness before you go into the room.

If your argument is quite weak or your statistics not thorough it's better to know this beforehand when you still have a chance to do something about it.

Remember my stricture about not being surprised in a negotiation. Try to construct every argument that the other party might put forward and try to predict the rebuttal that they're going to use on your argument. Run them past your team and ensure that you're well prepared.

Forewarned here is definitely forearmed.

Earn the outcome

One of the nicest compliments I've had over the years was when a client said, *"Tom, it was worth your fee just to see the look on their faces..."*

What this meant was that we were very well prepared, thorough and solid, while the other side had just turned up for a friendly chat, unprepared and without a clue what was going to happen.

I'll repeat a well-used mantra...if anything ever happens to you unexpectedly in a negotiation...blame yourself for your poor preparation. You should have predicted it.

You can't do this in the taxi on the way to the venue. If a deal starts to use words like 'millions' or 'key product' or 'strategic supplier' and you're not spending hours preparing for the meeting then frankly you deserve all you get...and you'll generally get nothing but grief and unhappiness.

You've been warned.

Keep the score

One of the advantages of a team negotiation is that you can have a scorekeeper. This is a vital role.

When a deal starts to become complicated with dozens of variables and large and complex calculations it's good to have someone whose sole role is to sit back and keep track of the numbers and the ebb and flow of the concessions.

This allows the people who are leading the negotiation to push forward with the logic and the trading without needing to stop to keep writing down the details. Obviously they must have a grip on the numbers but this is often done via a time out. The scorekeeper has the 'right' to call a time out if they feel that the numbers are going awry or that the deal is not moving according to plan.

It's a whole lot easier to sort out the problems in the privacy of a break-out room than to be hesitant in the meeting room because there's a misunderstanding about the numbers, clauses or details.

The scorekeeper is often the most experienced person in the team. Their position is to take the overview and manage the process and the numbers and let others do the arguing and bargaining.

Make the first speech

One of the most successful negotiations that I have been involved with occurred when my team took great advantage of playing the home game and opened up with a welcoming speech.

They courteously thanked the supplier for arriving and then took the opportunity to set the scene.

We'd rehearsed this part of the meeting...we even wrote the script and videoed the team leader while he practised his words.

Suffice it to say that this opening speech set such a powerful tone and created so much advantage that the whole of the rest of the day was spent literally sailing along.

Always try to get in the first blow in the fight. Make the first speech. Turn a courtesy into an advantage...set the scene and create a sense of power and authority that should give you the momentum throughout the meeting.

These first minutes are vitally important. You should plan for them meticulously.

Cover all the bases

People who know me will readily understand that I am not a detail person. I can live quite easily with overviews and leave the details to others.

Obviously this can be a weakness in a negotiation so I always ensure that I have with me (whenever possible) someone who can get serious with the calculator and the spreadsheet.

In any negotiation you need a set of roles and players who can fit them. If you don't possess certain traits that are important in creating a deal ensure that the team covers your weaknesses.

A good team covers all the bases and knows its strengths and weaknesses. Part of your preparation and planning should be a thorough audit of the team, the roles to be played, a learning of the script and a readiness for team action.

Good teams need thoughtful preparation...and it takes time.

Split the team

I was helping a client with a difficult negotiation recently and we spent some time looking at the other party.

There was going to be six of them and they formed a consortium who were bidding for a contract.

We looked closely at each member of the other party and tried to find their power rating in comparison with their colleagues; whether they'd formed any alliances within the consortium; who was the weakest link and who was the key influencer and decision maker.

We then looked at each of their negotiating styles and tried to predict how they'd behave and what particular elements of the deal would appeal to them and what particular style we could use to get our message across effectively to each of them.

The client wasn't used to spending so much time looking so closely at the other team but as subsequent events proved our insights were well worth the effort.

Never forget that a negotiation is an intensely personal exercise. Don't lose track of the other party and keep them in your mind in terms of how you can shape your arguments and run the meeting to suit your position and give you the best advantage.

Prepare for battle

I received an email from a delegate on a recent programme who told me that he'd managed to save more than he'd ever expected in a negotiation courtesy of my training.

It was very flattering, of course, but the key issue wasn't that he was now much more skilful or more tricky, it was purely that I'd told him to spend more time thinking about the negotiation in advance and to ensure that the negotiation was properly planned.

He could have done this without attending the programme but I'll take the credit nonetheless!

There's an old saying in negotiation:

To fail to prepare is to prepare to fail.

It's a bit trite, I know, but if your preparation has previously been in the taxi on the way to the negotiation then just ask yourself how much better your performance would be if you only got your ideas properly sorted in advance with a well-drawn-up battle plan.

Give it a try…your performance is bound to improve.

Set targets, walk aways and milestones

Athletes are good role models for negotiators. They are fit, they practise a lot and they have measured standards and targets.

Very few runners will have a target that is not very closely defined. They are not trying to run 'as fast as possible' but trying to beat 50 seconds for the 400 metres or run a marathon is less than four hours.

These are the targets that a good negotiator should have. By all means go for the 'Wow!!' but you must be able to put a number against what it looks like. For every variable you must have a range and a measurable set of numbers against each one.

We teach negotiators to be ambitious and persistent but they must be able to calibrate that persistence against measurable targets at every stage of the process.

Create your targets, walk aways and then put in the intermediate milestones. That way you'll always be in control of the journey and be able to measure your success properly.

Scope the opportunities

There are few activities in life where people are spontaneously excellent. If someone asks you the question: *"Can you play the piano?"* the answer, *"I don't know, I've never tried,"* may make them laugh but it is not an acceptable answer.

Few people can negotiate by just turning up, lifting the keyboard and starting to play.

Negotiation needs thought, practice and preparation. It is a dereliction of duty to attend a negotiation without having spent the appropriate time scoping the opportunities, thinking about the issues and people involved and setting targets and objectives. Negotiation is never a casual chat. It is a very structured event that requires pre-planning.

The next time you buy expensive tickets for a music concert just hope that the musician performing has been practising recently and isn't just trusting to luck.

Value the variables

I teach the importance of variables in our programmes. We teach identifying them and having a range for each one with proper 'Wow' positions and prepared intermediate markers.

We also teach that variables must be valued.

It's impossible to trade a variable if you don't know how much it's worth. Extending a warranty may be a reasonable concession to trade but not if you don't know the difference in value to you between a three-year warranty and a five-year version. You could easily find that you're giving away an enormously valuable concession and in return you are receiving very little.

So the next time you do your preparation ensure that you put a price tag against every one of your variables, valued by both yourself and how you think the other party might see it.

Also look at what you think the other party might trade and put a value on that also.

If you do this you'll always be sure of trading something cheap and getting some more valuable in return.

Look creatively for alternatives

When you walk into the negotiating room having a battery of alternatives with you will give you power.

The first alternative will be a BATNA (Best Alternative to No Agreement) which is well known among negotiators and is often referred to as a fire exit…a way out if all else fails.

Other alternatives are those parts of the deal that can be sacrificed if necessary. It always helps not to have 'do or die' situations in a deal and flexibility gives you options.

You should also be aware of what options the other party may have, how they can present them to you and what they may consider as acceptable.

The greater the ability of both sides to look creatively at alternatives the greater the ability to create value and seek a lasting positive solution.

If you are in a go/no go situation realise your potential weakness and try to ensure that you don't place yourself in an untenable position. That may be easier said than done but it's an important principle.

Show discipline and control

I was working with a team of buyers recently and we spent a day getting ready to do battle.

I taught them that they should have an agenda, that they should be well rehearsed and they should have good teamwork...not interrupting and ensuring that each member knew their role, when to speak and just as importantly when to remain quiet.

The comparison with the two large multinational sales teams was remarkable. The other side were ill prepared, didn't know their figures, had no idea of teamwork and in short were a rabble.

You don't have to be a world beater to be a good negotiator. You only need to be better than the other side and the good news is that in many cases the other side is pretty useless.

So do your homework, keep it simple, have an agenda, create good teamwork and reap the rewards.

Take control

The more that I look at preparation in negotiation the more I realise the need to remain in control of the total process.

This includes pre-meeting conditioning, the agenda, the organisation and the flow of the meeting.

Of these I would identify the first opening statement as the key issue. If you open the meeting with a powerful statement and introduce your key points, the whole tone of the meeting is in your favour.

This obviously favours the buyer who is often playing the home game and as such can begin with a welcoming and conditioning speech.

Sellers may need to start the process earlier so that they can score their points before the meeting even begins. That's the power of conditioning.

Nothing should ever happen by chance in a well-planned negotiation.

Plan strategically

I was asked this week to help solve a negotiation problem which was basically unsolvable.

A monopolist was abusing their position in the market-place and offering a 'take it or leave it' argument to a major client.

Negotiation can add enormous value to any business scenario but when it is applied it represents essentially a tactical solution to a situation that should have been strategically planned.

There's no magic dust here. If you have a strategic market problem it's going to require strategic solutions. Plan to change the market or plan to change the buyer/seller power balance and then and only then ask negotiation to help you achieve it.

Have high hopes

You get some very odd looks from people when you say that you can save them 50% on a deal.

"It can't be done," or *"That's incredible,"* are frequent responses.

Real evidence proves that deals can be enhanced by 10s of per cents if you're a buyer or seller by just asking, pure and simple. It's a matter of ambition.

If you're a buyer why not look at the marginal costings and forget the fixed costs (that's for the other customers!)?

If you're a seller look at the new variables that you never even considered and get the extra value added that creative negotiating provides.

If you don't ask, you don't get.

If you ask for a little, you'll get a little.

If you ask for a lot, you'll get a whole lot more.

Plan for and predict problems

People often ask, *"What do you think I should do in this situation?"* They then tell me a complicated tale of woe involving errors and difficulties that far better people than I would find impossible to solve.

The answer is generally something like, *"If I were you I wouldn't get myself in that sort of position."*

That's not a smart consultant answer but a genuine feeling that you can't heal a strategic wound with a tactical bandage.

Strategic problems don't just happen, they develop. Serious preparation and scenario planning ensure that most contingencies will be covered before they happen and cause problems.

A problem predicted and planned for is a problem half solved.

Read the small print

In the retail world *"Let the buyer beware"* is a well-known maxim. In fact it is not really a problem as most shops will offer a refund if a genuine mistake is made. They wouldn't wish to lose the goodwill.

Negotiations are rather different. Relying on the goodwill of the other party could be a very naïve strategy so you should be well prepared. Check the terms and conditions very carefully. Ensure that there is nothing that will return to bite you after you've signed.

Of course you can then decide what you would do if you noticed a palpable error on the other side. Is it good business or bad, will it help foster the relationship or not, will you see these people again?

The choice is yours!

Always have options

Desperate people pay desperate prices. People who 'must have' that apartment of their dreams pay a hefty premium because they won't walk away.

Ensure that you always have options. Do your 'what if' planning and always have a back door to the deal. There are very, very few 'must have' products or services (unless you are a five-year old at Christmas!).

If you know you can walk away with a smile then you can negotiate with an even mind and let the other party do the worrying.

Choose the right words

In a recent UK-based negotiation the other party made a claim that they were expecting to receive *"value up to a certain amount"* which they named.

This short sentence contained at least three weaknesses.

The first is that they immediately put down a marker and limited their ambition by naming the amount.

The second is that they used the word *"value"*. This told the other party that they didn't have to pay cash and other means would be acceptable.

The third and worst error was the word *"to"*. This meant that they were prepared to accept LESS than their stated number. The expression, *"a minimum of"* would have been so much stronger.

Choose your words carefully. The other side is listening!

Understand the human dimension

People rightly say that the internet has made markets more competitive and that buyers can go online to check the best deals.

In just a matter of minutes you can compare Gateway's prices with Dell's, match the specifications and know who offers the best-value computer.

There's just one small problem. You're comparing list prices with list prices. Computers can't give you a discount and computers can't use their discretion to add in a service at a reduced price.

Don't lose sight of the human dimension. By all means compare prices but then speak to a real person...you might be pleasantly surprised.

Establish trust up front

In any negotiation you'll need to decide how much
you're going to have to trust the other side. You've
got to work out whether they're telling lies, offering
exaggerations or telling the truth.

They're doing the same about you.

Have an open mind. Most experts tell you to be entirely
suspicious until you have evidence to the contrary. That
can be a time-consuming and often cynical position.

Try to establish trust right up front. Spend some time
with trust on your agenda and then, with some of the
relationship issues resolved, you'll know how to behave
best when the money is on the table.

Concentrate on strengths

People often go into negotiations absolutely convinced that they are in a terrible position and that the other party has all the power and advantage.

Ironically you often find that the other party is sitting across the table thinking exactly the same thing.

Power is never absolute and is always a matter of perception. If you believe that you are in a weak position you will behave accordingly. If you believe that you have options and are empowered then your confidence levels will soar.

Always concentrate on your strengths and the other party's weaknesses (they will have some). That way you maintain advantage and build confidence.

The hole is never as deep as you think it is.

Show clarity of interest

In a negotiation you've generally got two choices to make for both the outcome and the relationship.

You can choose to claim the value that is being negotiated or you can choose to create new value. This means that you can either decide to play tough and get a short-term advantage or you can try to take a longer view and maybe build a relationship.

What you do need to know is how you're going to have to behave in order to achieve your aim.

Don't enter a negotiation without an understanding of how you intend to behave and what influence this will have on both the short-term acquisition of value and the longer-term building of a relationship.

Have a long list of variables

Every training course on negotiation contains a section on variables. These are the negotiation items that you are able to exchange in return for other advantages.

It may be that you would be prepared to vary the price in return for more volume or a longer contract. That makes price, volume and contract length three key variables.

You must never go into a negotiation without a long list of these tradable items. We routinely find at least 50 variables before we ever enter the negotiating room.

Variables make a deal complex and their parameters need to be scoped but if you have them in your possession then you'll always have an answer to a tough problem and you'll almost never reach deadlock.

3

Negotiation Philosophy

I've read many books over the years and listened to many tapes. I always try to summarise the best ideas and communicate them in the tips.

Here are some interesting principles and good ideas that I've come across.

Always look closely

It is often said that owners and their dogs eventually start to look alike.

People who spend time together often start to share similar views and reactions to situations. In selling this is called 'going native' and that's why many sales organisations will rotate their sales teams after a couple of years because the seller starts to get too close to the customer and loses their objective focus.

Many negotiators meet the same people many times over long periods and it's reasonable to suggest that after a period of acquaintance and maybe friendship there exists a coming together of feelings and attitudes. This is called emotional convergence.

This is not a bad thing if the convergence is towards creativity and value creating. It is certainly not a bonus if both sides have converged towards a hostile and mutually disrespectful position.

As you meet people over a period of time you have the opportunity to shape their expectations of you and manage their reactions to your regular comments and business practices.

Very little happens by chance in a negotiation. Take a close look at yourself and the other party and see if any learned responses are in play...and ask if they are positive or negative.

Never explain...

There's a saying in politics:

"Never explain, never apologise."

Let's examine this in the field of negotiation. What we wish to achieve as serious negotiators is a good outcome and we're going to be more likely to achieve it if the other side respects us or in some cases fears us.

As always you'll hear me offer the caveat that we never wish to jeopardise a strong business relationship but we also don't want to 'buy' that relationship at too high a price.

There are fine lines to be drawn between confidence and arrogance and between respect and dislike so let's get the definitions clear:

We need to look confident and powerful.

We need the other side to respect us and to be on their guard.

We need to ensure that we never look weak.

We need to make it seem that we have many choices.

I'd suggest a role model for this style was Mrs Thatcher: a woman many people disliked but nobody took for granted. Respect and fear went often hand in hand.

How does the other party view you?

Reciprocate

The tit-for-tat strategy is a favourite of mine.

In posher language it is the behaviour of total reciprocity. It says to the other party that you will mirror their behaviour absolutely so how they behave to you will become the way you behave to them.

This appeals to me. I'll be good to you...if you reciprocate then I'll reciprocate...and so on.

If I'm good to you and you're bad to me...then I'll be bad to you back (with maybe a little bit of interest!) as a disincentive to future bad behaviour.

Remember how you bring up your kids. You reward their good behaviour and punish their bad behaviour. Negotiation isn't much different.

Seize the day!

I believe in a very cooperative negotiation style. I see
no reason to cause unhappiness and grief...it's both bad
for business and bad for the relationship...and that's
what secures future business.

EXCEPT

Assume I'm never going to see you again. Assume you're
a stranger selling me a car or buying my house.

I believe the rules are different here. If it's a one-
shot negotiation without any consequences for the
relationship then you can go for broke and compete for
all your worth.

You can make your own moral decisions about what's
fair and what's not but the key concept is that when
you've only got one shot at the target make sure it's
your best shot and don't be too precious about the
other party...they're probably doing the same to you.

Go for it.

Form coalitions

Big Brother and other reality shows on television have shown us clearly how important it is to get on with people when you're working in a team.

In *Big Brother* the participants are asked to nominate two people to kick off and the audience then votes.

The secret is not to be selected by your housemates and one of the most effective ways of doing this is to form small coalitions of groups with a common purpose.

This is not a Machiavellian concept of playing people off against each other but a legitimate attempt to form those around you into groups of people who see you as a friend or ally. The office is an obvious example of how you'll find yourself in several different coalitions based on your work and social drivers.

People who don't live within coalitions are outsiders... and while it's often good to live on the outside remember that outsiders don't have influence and influence is what we're trying to achieve if we want to be an effective negotiator.

Reap what is sown

I don't nanny the readers in these tips. You're all able to develop your own moral code and decide what's a legitimate tactic and what's a dirty trick; when to tell the truth and when to say nothing; when to look for a win/win solution and when to go for broke.

These are the daily decisions of every negotiator and I leave those decisions to you.

What I do urge…and you can disregard it if you wish… is to remember that what goes around comes around.

People have long memories and if you work a fast one on the other party to secure a short-term advantage you can rest assured that they'll want their revenge some time soon.

I live in a part of the word where favours are a negotiable commodity…you help me…I'll help you. That's a code I like…I'll make the first step…I'll trust you and then I'll reciprocate your behaviour. Treat me well and we're friends…treat me otherwise and tighten your seatbelt.

Map out the influencers

One of the reasons that I don't much like political or trade union negotiations is because of the power and interference of third parties.

In a buyer/seller relationship we have essentially two parties...and they're sitting opposite each other across the table.

At an industrial relations negotiation the bosses have to answer to the board and the unions need to get their membership to sign off. This often means that most of the negotiations are not with the principals of the negotiation but with the secondary parties.

Political negotiations are even more complex. The media have an axe to grind, the voters are factored in (nobody wants to lose an election) and you can list a whole host of interested parties.

If you do have complex negotiations ensure that you understand the power of the third parties. You'll need to map out the influencers and create a strategy to deal with them.

It's just so much easier if the decision makers are sitting right opposite you across the table...but sometimes that's a luxury that we just don't have.

Know the moves

Students on my training programmes often ask what they might do if they meet somebody who has also been trained to negotiate. They fear a stand-off and stalemate.

My experience is totally the opposite. When I'm dealing with professionals I know that the process will be smoother and will 'cut to the chase' more quickly in a more focused manner.

The pros don't try to use cheap tricks because they know they won't work and usually they also understand the power of time and opportunity cost so nobody wants the process to drag on endlessly.

So don't fear dealing with an experienced negotiator. The process should prove far simpler than you think. Remember this analogy with chess…grandmasters know the moves and they move quickly…only novices waste time with poor moves. Usually the start of a chess match is very well known and easy to execute…it's only 20 moves into the game that the complexities really begin to become apparent and the real pros start to operate…that's the part of the negotiation you want to get to quickly because that's where the real value will be created.

Get results and get along

I always try to start my training programmes with a definition of what negotiation is and how it is managed.

There are many different definitions but let's try another one here…

Negotiation is about reaching an agreement with someone with whom you disagree. It could be a company, a person…anyone with whom you wish to move forward together…anyone where you have had conflict…and you wish to end that conflict…and replace it with a more positive and joint way forward… they're the consequences of the deal.

In short we're keen to do a deal and manage the relationship…getting what you want and getting along with people. These are the two powerful and simultaneous activities of the experienced negotiator.

Make the right decision

What is your objective in a negotiation? Is it to win...to make money...or maybe just to survive?

Here's a generic objective...your task in a negotiation is to make the right decision. If you continue to make right decisions you'll succeed in the long run even if in the short run you get a little bruised.

Remember that over a lifetime of negotiation you're going to make thousands of decisions. Some of them will be hugely important and some quite trivial...what matters is that you always try to make the right decision when you're faced with it.

Be thoughtful...take a pause...weigh the issues and the consequences...make the best decision you can and then pursue it with vigour.

You might even take this as a life skill...but then negotiation is all about life...isn't it?

Take the robust approach

If you're interested in negotiation you should read anything that Danny Ertel writes. He understands the topic very well.

Here's a quote from him from the *Harvard Business Review*:

"A strong relationship creates trust, which allows the parties to share information more freely, which in turn leads to more creative and valuable agreements and a willingness to continue working together. But when a deal is struck that is not very attractive to one or both parties, chances are that they will invest less time and effort in working together, they will become more wary in communicating with each other and their relationship will grow strained."

This is just the dilemma a client of mine is facing with a longstanding customer who wants to reduce the price of their work. They don't want to say *"No"* but they don't want to damage the relationship.

It shouldn't be too hard to manage an assertive negotiation of the deal without jeopardising the relationship. In fact a robust negotiation can often improve a relationship…not harm it. If you give in too quickly the other party may not respect you and you'll find that next time they'll be back for even more.

Show awareness and realism

In the movie *Somethin's Gotta Give*, Jack Nicholson says to Diane Keaton:

"I have never lied to you. I have always told you some version of the truth."

What a negotiator this man is!

Lying, as I've said many times in these tips, is definitely incorrect, immoral and capable of destroying relationships. That much I can tell you easily.

I can't be so categorical about being 'economical with the truth' or which version of truth to tell.

So let's not get too hung up about this. Let's remember that truth is a complicated issue and while the other party may not be lying to you, a great deal of varnish might be put on their truth or a great dose of hyperbole could also be included.

Just be aware…and sensible…and a little realistic.

Go to the edge

When you're in a negotiation you need to know where the zone is. The zone is the area of overlap between you and the other party which is pretty much the destination for the final agreement.

If there's no zone...there will probably be no agreement.

Successful negotiators go one better. They get into the zone with the other party but then they get to the edge of the zone. It's the edge where the best deals are to be found.

Don't just settle for an easy deal...a simple overlap of objectives. What you need to do is to get to the edge... find out how much extra you can obtain without jeopardising the future relationship.

In any deal there is always extra to be made by stretching the elastic a bit more...by seeing if you can get an extra step towards the edge before it gets too dangerous.

If you can get to this edge then you'll be in negotiation heaven...the nirvana of success where winners get.... FREE MONEY.

Smile and say "*thank you*"

I have authored the occasional idea and phrase but one I'm very proud of is: *"Nice is good for business."*

I use this expression on all my programmes and endeavour to tell people why it is that making enemies in business is bad for the bottom line and why if people like you they will throw their cash in your direction.

It's not exactly the theory of relativity but it works. If people meet you and they're looking for revenge as a result of the last meeting then two things will happen: you'll have a sour meeting and it'll cost you money.

If people come to the meeting with warm feelings about how you treated them before then you're on the way before you've even started.

Never believe that the best negotiators are fierce table bangers. It couldn't be further from the truth.

Be nice to people...and smile and say *"thank you"* every time they give you some of their money.

Understand the value equation

I bang on about value a lot in my seminars. It's a key principle in business negotiation and represents in a nutshell the reason why everyone is at the table.

It's very easy to equate value with money. Business negotiation invariably has price and cost at its heart but there are many other concerns.

Value may be the management of risk...the most effective use of time...the creation of goodwill...the number of people involved in the project...the sharing of resource...and the list goes on.

You will know how bargaining takes the heat out of price. That's the value equation and value doesn't necessarily mean lowest price at all.

I remember a tender where the highest bidder won. The reason was because they could do the job fastest and in this particular environment time was very much of the essence.

At the highest price they represented the best value. People sometimes need persuading about this but remember price and value are not always neighbours in the deal.

Never lose sight of the solution

People only negotiate with people who disagree with them. If they didn't disagree they wouldn't have anything to negotiate about.

At the same time people only negotiate with people with whom they want to have an agreement with... otherwise they wouldn't bother to invest the time and energy.

So on one hand we have disagreement but at the same time we have a strong urge to reach a conclusion. We only argue with our potential friends. That's the irony.

This is the topic that Roger Fisher and William Ury have discussed so well in their various books. The desire to negotiate to reach a position that helps both parties while at the same time closing the initial gap that created the need for negotiation in the first place.

Never let the difference...the gap...become more important than the solution. Once a negotiation turns into trench warfare then the solution gets lost amidst the noise of battle and the smell of gunpowder.

If it's in your interests to reach a deal then fix it. Don't let the initial gap put you off. Obviously it takes two to tango...and if the other party won't play then you'll never succeed but if both parties show goodwill there's no gap that can't be closed in favour of a positive outcome.

Use impartial advice

I'm not one to bang the drum about consultancy services...in fact I believe that in many cases clients could do just as well without them. (It was painful to write that sentence!)

The one area where consultancy can help in a negotiation is in the area of impartial advice and third-party support.

It can be extremely valuable to have somebody question the status quo, ask naïve questions, challenge the perceived wisdom and make suggestions from outside the frame of reference.

One reply that I receive over and over again from clients is *"Well, that's the way we've always done it..."* I asked one client why they weren't asking for a longer warranty period and the reply was: *"Well, three years is our standard period."* My reply was: *"Why?"*

We ended up with a seven-year warranty because I asked for more and challenged a perceived status quo.

Maybe you still don't need a consultant. Maybe you can invite in to the team a colleague from your own company...but remember that in most cases a fresh pair of eyes and a fresh intellect can work wonders.

Use all the channels

Negotiation channels can take place in several different ways. Let's examine three.

The front channel for a negotiation is the main room where the key players are negotiating the substantive deal. This negotiation may or may not hinge on their ability to sell the deal to their constituent parties and on this basis the deal progresses.

The back channel of a negotiation exists when the key players set up a separate team to negotiate an issue within the deal that may take place in parallel with the substantive deal. This second room often gets going on a tough issue that has caused deadlock in the main room. On this basis they then report back, ideally with a solution.

The third channel of a negotiation involves outsiders. These may be experts, not part of the original team, who are drafted in to help solve a particular issue. These are often of a technical nature. In their role as technical advisors their task is to fix the problem rather than worry about the substantive deal which may still be continuing in the main room.

Don't limit yourself to just one channel. When the going gets tough you may find some extra channels to be helpful.

Avoid auctions

There are different types of auction.

First is the open outcry English auction where the highest bidder wins.

Second is the Dutch auction where in a dropping price the first bidder wins.

Third is the sealed bid auction...highest bidder wins.

All of these have flaws for the keen negotiator. In the English version there's the problem of making the sale to a bidder who would have gone higher if the second bidder hadn't dropped out.

In the Dutch version as buyers we climb a wall of worry hoping the price will go down further but dreading a winning bid by another player.

In the sealed bid version as sellers we've got a real issue of playing against people who'll not bid too high fearful of overbidding and then being 'clarified' downwards. Collusion is also a real problem if parties talk beforehand or have similar market knowledge.

It seems to me that a two-party negotiation beats all three of these methods of buying and selling.

Focus on bigger slices

One of the dilemmas that a negotiator always has is whether they should go for a bigger slice of the current pie or seek to create a larger pie which will then hopefully give them an even larger slice.

In every negotiation the creation of value is linked absolutely to the claiming of value.

If you go for a larger slice and so does the other party then the pie might actually shrink and then you'd be even worse off.

You and the other party are interdependent and with a bit of common sense it should be easy to maximise the joint payoff and each party gets a bigger slice. The alternative is to get so much process loss and conflict in the deal that the pie shrinks visibly in front of you.

Remember that the answer is not if you got a bigger slice than the other party but whether you maximised the slice that was available to you. Pyrrhic victories are failures and wars of attrition are also failures. Success is bigger slices for you...just don't worry about the other party's slice size...that's their problem. They'll soon tell you if they're unhappy.

Keep the other side on their toes

When we discuss trust we often think that people who are unpredictable are hard to trust. Most people like to be able to predict people's behaviour because it makes their life easier.

You can trust a thief to steal your wallet and you can trust an honest person to give it back. The real problem is with people who sometimes do one thing and sometimes do the other. It's hard dealing with these people…you're not sure how to behave.

Ironically this is just the right sort of behaviour for a successful negotiator. You need to be just predictable enough for the other party to be able to trust what you say but you need to be unpredictable enough to prevent them reading your every move.

Negotiators who are predictable are like chess players who always use the same opening and the same attacking formations. Their opponents quickly find out how to deal with them.

So...let's keep the other side on their toes...but not at the expense of the trust that we need to build up to make the deal work.

It's an interesting balance.

Understand and use game theory

There are many academic definitions of game theory. In short and in practical terms it is a means by which individual people can make decisions based on the outcomes that they prefer and based on the actions that they believe the other party may also make.

The script is…*"I'll do X because they'll do Y and that'll be good for us…but if they were to vote X then I may consider a Y vote because that would give us the better outcome."*

The negotiator then goes away and plans for the contingencies and the consequences.

In a fully functioning negotiation process the above only happens when the other party doesn't wish to participate in a joint decision-making process. When negotiators really get together they can discuss the options and the consequences in plenary and joint sessions and therefore they can both understand the value-adding or value-reducing consequences of their joint actions.

In short...by all means prepare the possible action strategies before the meeting but before you make a decision be very sure that the other party understands all the issues and shares your view of the pluses or minuses of the outcomes.

Collaboration and openness have to be the name of this game.

Make the best decisions jointly

Let's follow the thread of the last couple of tips and see how the ability to make decisions jointly is better than the game theory issues of separate decision making.

The first issue is that you can now make decisions that have joint payoffs that are mutually agreed.

The second issue is that you can communicate with each other about what your wants and needs are... honestly or not.

Lastly you can be creative and move beyond go/no go decisions.

These three items represent the foundation for collaborative negotiation.

It shouldn't be hard to imagine the value and synergy that can be created by mutually agreed outcomes with joint benefits based on creative decisions.

Sad to say, despite the obvious benefits many parties will still seek to play a high-leverage go/no go game with little communication and no creativity.

You can't force people to collaborate...but you'd have to be very sure indeed that your personal individual solution was so good that you couldn't see any value in talking and collaborating with the other party.

I leave the decision to you.

Use soft power

I was listening to a political interview. The subject was the use of power and the speaker talked about hard power and soft power.

Hard power is the naked use of force...in political terms it means the use of military, unilateral force to win a battle. In commercial terms it will mean the use of absolute threat on a *"Take it or suffer the consequences"* basis.

You don't need to be an expert to see how relationships suffer in this respect.

Soft power is the use of collaborative persuasion to bring people round to your point of view willingly. Politically this is the need for consensus at the United Nations. Commercially it is the ability to solve problems jointly and create a mutually enhancing solution.

The thesis of the speaker was that hard power alone is not enough...you need to use it in concert with soft power if you wish to achieve your goals and maintain relationships.

Raise the IQ

I often define persuasion as the ability to turn a *"No"* into a *"Yes"*.

Imagine a world full of happy people all agreeing with you...kids going to bed on time...bosses giving you a raise...colleagues sharing resources.

Sadly it's not very common. We live in a world where people quite often don't agree with us and don't wish to do what we want and give us what we think is fair. That's when it's important to be able use persuasion and influence.

People with a high Influence Quotient (and I'm very happy to say that it's a phrase that I've invented) generally get more than their 'fair' share and are always likely to rise to the top of the heap.

If your life is full of negatives, *"No"* replies, refusals and a general lack of resource then you might like to explore how you could increase your negotiation horsepower and raise your Influence Quotient.

Avoid revenge

I quite like the idea that you can only negotiate with another party once, and that's the first time. The second time that you meet them it's not a negotiation, more a furthering of the ongoing relationship.

People will bring all manner of baggage into the negotiation room from previous meetings and if you've treated them badly or they perceive that they have been badly done by then you'll find that they will be out for revenge. Trying to negotiate with people looking for revenge is a very tough issue indeed.

I like the idea of creating a win/win relationship in my negotiations. A win/win relationship is where both parties treat each other with respect and that the relationship becomes mutually enhancing. This has nothing to do with the division or creation of the value (I have certain misgivings about win/win negotiations) but it does say a lot about the way we handle people.

A phrase I've used a lot recently is *"Nice is good for business"*.

I like negotiators I train to be OK people...easy to get on with, pleasant and friendly folks. The reason is that this is the best means to find your way to the pot of gold which is the outcome you desire.

Bend with the breeze

I was asked this week to offer some advice to somebody who found themselves getting angry with the other party during a negotiation.

It seems that they were getting riled by a few smart comments and wanted to hit back with even smarter comments. I cautioned against this because if you raise the temperature in a negotiation you'll soon find that the other party has raised it even more and the next thing you'll know is that you're in a blazing row.

This is what Neil Rackham calls the 'Defend-Attack Spiral'.

These days, now that I'm a little older and wiser, I prefer to smile and let the other party's behaviour wash over me. Certainly I'll try to save my anger for outside the negotiating room.

Be calm, take the blame on yourself if necessary to defuse the situation but ensure that you get even. Sadly I'm not a pacifist here. Let's not get mad…for sure…but let's equally be sure that we get even!

Anger and hurt pride can be expensive luxuries in a negotiation.

N.B. I'm trying hard to take my own medicine!

Use short-term tactics with care

I want to repeat a point I'm sure I've made many times before but it bears repetition. Any fool can strike a good short-term deal by destroying relationships and leveraging the opportunity.

I teach many tactics and a tactic well used can lubricate a negotiation and help it on its way. A manipulative tactic used to score a cheap short-term point will certainly gain the user an advantage but the consequences are pretty poor when the victim wises up and realises what has been done to them.

Revenge is not a pleasant sight...if you're on the wrong side of the table. So...let's remember, we want a good deal this week and an even better deal next week. Let's get great value in the short term and foster good relationships in the long term.

That's got to be the best recipe. Tactics are fine but like chilli powder we need just enough for taste...too much burns!

Avoid the sucker's choice

I came across the expression 'sucker's choice' recently and liked the concept and thought how apt is was when thinking about negotiation.

There are many situations where you are given a choice by the other party along the lines of *"Take it or leave it"* or something like *"Well, do you want it or not?"*

These are often at the end of a difficult and heated session when people are saying quite extreme things and putting the pressure on the other party.

A forced choice is being offered of two extreme and mutually exclusive positions.

This is the sucker's choice. If you ever believe that there are only two choices you are limiting yourself way beyond what's possible and even sensible.

Recently George Bush said about terrorism: *"You're either with us or against us"*. Well that's not exactly the full picture. It is quite reasonable to be fully anti-terrorism without necessarily accepting that the George Bush position is the best one. It's not either north or south…there are many compass positions in between.

Don't ever allow yourself to be painted into this sort of corner where you only have two forced options... generally created by the other party.

Give yourself freedom and allow yourself to follow a route that fully gives you latitude and flexibility.

Bargain

There are two types of bargaining that are common within negotiation theory. One is distributive bargaining, the other integrative bargaining.

Distributive bargaining involves one side having goals that are in direct conflict with the other party. Resources are limited and the argument concerns who will get the larger share of the pie. Essentially it's a zero sum game.

Integrative bargaining implies that the pie is not limited and it is not a zero sum game. It suggests:

A focus on commonalities rather than differences.

An attempt to address needs and interest rather than positions.

A commitment to meeting the needs of all parties.

An exchange of information and ideas.

The invention of options for mutual gain.

The use of objective criteria for standards of performance.

Circumstances will always dictate the correct approach but I would suggest that life as a distributive bargainer can be very hard work if you see every deal as a battle to be won rather than an opportunity to create value.

Keep the process going

I find Roger Dawson's definition of the three problems of impasse, stalemate and deadlock very helpful:

Impasse: you are in complete disagreement on one issue that is threatening to derail the whole negotiation.

Stalemate: both sides are still talking but seem unable to make any substantive progress.

Deadlock: the lack of progress has frustrated each side so much that they see little reason to continue the negotiation.

Here are the solutions:

If you have an impasse then put it to one side and continue with the easy stuff so that you can maintain momentum. You can then come back to the roadblock later but don't narrow it down to just that one issue or you'll make it a deal breaker.

If you have a stalemate then it's time to change one of the elements of the negotiation. Change the people, venue, ease the tension, share the feelings.

If you have a deadlock then it's time for a third party or arbitrator. Don't be afraid of a deadlock. If you're afraid of a deadlock you'll give up a valuable advantage. There's no problem in bringing in a neutral outsider who can add fresh perspectives.

Sort out your own ethical code

The approach that I teach contains many different types of tactics which, when used effectively, can help facilitate the negotiation process and offer real advantage.

The Building Block tactic for buyers is a powerful way of putting your business into the marketplace in stages. For sellers the Package Deal is a legitimate means of presenting a full service option to the customer.

There are, however, several grey areas where legitimate tactics like these become rank dirty tricks and can damage relationships. The problem is that I'm not sure where this line is drawn.

Is it a legitimate tactic to say to the other party, *"This is the best I can do..."* when you know that you could offer more?

Is it appropriate to tell a supplier that you'll take your business elsewhere if you don't get a reduction when you know that you'd never do such a thing?

I have enough trouble sorting out my own ethical code without trying to tell others what's ethical and what's not. You'll have to decide that for yourself and then decide whether 'your final offer' really is final or whether it's a legitimate phrase to use in the heat of the battle, or whether it's a lie.

Your choice.

Use your common sense

I was running a training seminar recently for a client who was particularly cost conscious. They checked every aspect of the venue and what was being offered.

They noticed that bottles of mineral water were part of the daily offering. They just as readily noticed that the delegates were not drinking all the water each day.

As cynical and careful money managers they marked some of the bottles and noticed that the very same bottles appeared on the following day and therefore the venue was charging multiple times for the selfsame bottles of water.

When approached the venue said that the water was a standard part of the package and as such was non-negotiable.

My client, distinctly unimpressed by this approach, decided to take action and at the end of day two opened each bottle and poured some water into glasses.

Accordingly on day three new and unopened bottles appeared and the client thought that at least they were getting new bottles instead of being 'cheated' by the old bottles being recycled.

Ask yourself if this is anything other than the logic of the madhouse. This is a perfect example of lose/lose negotiation. Water got wasted, money was spent needlessly and what's worse the relationship took a real step backwards. Both parties should have been locked up and forced to fix this issue properly.

Don't ever allow this to happen to you....please!

Learn to influence

I'm being asked by more and more organisations to provide negotiation classes form them internally. These are for employees who do not interface with the sellers or with clients but who need to provide services with colleagues and ensure that the resources that are required, usually people and time, are properly allocated. The human resource department comes often to mind.

These skills are often described as influencing skills rather than negotiating skills and I apply a slightly different model to this particular situation.

Influencing is the means by which one party seeks to create a situation whereby their opinions and ideas are readily accepted by the other party. This suggests an element of persuasion, of course, and maybe an element of selling (albeit of a concept rather than a product or service).

Normally my standard process works well in the majority of cases but it has been formulated to work very much within the context of buying and selling.

I adapt the commercial model to cover influencing by including more elements of communication, rapport building and personal authority, which are more in play in non-commercial situations.

Influencing is a more subtle art and requires a different approach to the dollars and cents world of commerce.

Stick to the rules

Influential people are able to bring to bear many different, effective techniques and behaviours so that their desired outcome prevails and so that the outcome of the transaction has a positive effect on the ongoing relationship.

Here is one of the most successful:

Legitimacy. Legitimacy is the technique of persuading the other party that they should comply with the desired outcome because that is the 'rule' and it should not be broken. Alan Funt, in a famous *Candid Camera* stunt, placed a sign on the freeway saying *"Delaware Closed"* and then watched as people turned around and accepted it absolutely.

If you can get people to believe that your way is the accepted way and to do it another way would be a breaking of the rules then you're in a strong position. People enjoy the continuance of the status quo and therefore you should try to suggest that doing it your way is merely a continuation of what is the accepted way of doing things as written down (or not) by the organisation.

"It's what would be acceptable here according to our rules and policies," is a good starting script for the use of legitimacy.

This then makes a different strategy look risky and *ultra vires* in terms of the organisation's principles and procedures. The technique of legitimacy works particularly well in countries where people are culturally conditioned to follow the rules rather than to wish to break them.

Find the authority

You will find it easier to influence people if you demonstrate two important personal characteristics:

Expertise. We've grown up in the media age listening to experts who tell us what to do and in many cases we meekly follow. We believe our doctor when they tell us that we need to do something. We follow the advice absolutely. They're the experts, not us!

In a more unscrupulous environment bogus car mechanics have caused customers to spend more money than was needed because their diagnosis of the problem was believed.

So…if you want people to be influenced more readily by you it pays to tell them why you're an expert and they're not and if you can put your credentials and experience on the table they're going to find it very hard to combat your point.

Authority. Many people and societies are conditioned to follow the edicts and ideas of people and organisations that often take an authoritative stance. In the USA, if the FDA declares a drug to be unsafe then nobody will take it and it will immediately be removed from the shelves.

Their authority in this matter is absolute. Much the same occurs in the world of flying where the FAA controls what happens without argument.

If you wish to use authority then you need to find powerful and credible support for your argument and be able to show that strong and important people and credible sources have supported your position: accordingly your argument is the only acceptable way forward.

Show persistence

There are two other significant aspects of influence that need to be covered:

Precedent. Custom and practice are great ways to show people that your approach should be adopted. *"We've always done it like this in the past and it was successful so I suggest that we don't change a winning formula…"* is a fine script and likely to get precedent working well for you.

You can use a perceived threat that to do things differently (from previous practice) might not be such a good way forward and could cause upset. This tactic appeals to people's conservative nature and will be more powerful in organisations or cultures where the past is seen as a powerful template for the future.

Ironically some organisations may hold completely the opposite mindset so you need to play this card carefully.

Persistence. History is full of examples of people who failed and failed but still kept coming back for more until eventually their arguments prevailed.

You are never going to be influential unless you're prepared to accept that you cannot win every argument and that you may need to prepare a 'Plan B' in case you fail and need to take a new approach.

There is more than one way to be successful so if at first you don't succeed try again. The successful fisherman continues to throw his hook back into the water no matter how many times the fish don't bite. It's never a case of 'if' but only 'when'.

Understand what makes us tick

People won't 'buy' your argument or position unless they can see that it will help them in some way (that is easy to define).

Unless they either want it or need it they're going to find it very easy to reject what you have to say.

Your challenge as an influencer is to be able to wrap up your points so that they appeal to the other party in such a way that they can readily see what value and benefit your ideas will add to where they currently stand.

Being able to address people's hopes and fears will readily make this 'sale' more easy to make. It is often said that people are motivated to buy things through either fear or greed. If you can appeal to these two 'hot buttons' then you're not doing too badly. Underestimating human nature is cynical but often very profitable.

Understanding why someone should want to 'buy' your argument and then addressing that need is one of the key attributes of the successful and effective influencer.

Knowing your target audience and knowing what makes them tick is the first and most important starting point in the influencing process.

Accommodate but don't compromise

In the my model of negotiation I believe that a compromise is not a strong method of reaching agreement. We define a compromise as a matter of splitting differences…looking for the 50/50 choice.

This is often a very poor method of achieving agreement as it merely relies on each side being prepared to make concessions in order to reach a position that causes as little mutual pain as possible.

Nobody wins in a compromise. Everyone must lose by definition. All you get is an agreement (which may not be such a bad thing) but it's a poor man's way of negotiating.

I tend to use the word 'accommodation' to describe what others may mean by compromise.

An accommodation in my book is the means by which two parties reach an agreement that suits each party's personal or business needs in a fair and positive way.

It is not 50/50. It is more like 100/100 where each party gets what they want by bargaining and exchanging variables...maybe conceding here and there but gaining also here and there.

That's a decent agreement. An accommodation of differing objectives within a fair and reasonable agreement.

It is most certainly not a compromise.

Create value through win/win

I believe very strongly in win/win relationships. When we do business you treat me with respect and courtesy and I reciprocate. We feel that our relationship is growing and is likely to be enhanced by the deal and its outcomes.

Win/win negotiations are a slightly different piece of business. I believe in win/win when it comes to creating value: you pay me quickly and I give you a discount. That's win/win synergy.

What's slightly harder to map is the distribution of the value. Should we split the value 50/50? Did I take more risk? Did you use greater resources?

That's where win/win negotiation tends to fail. It tells us about collaborating to create value but doesn't have much to say about dividing that value. When we're faced with this problem we tend to fall back on the tried and tested win/perceived win formula whereby I achieve my objectives and you feel happy enough (but neither too happy nor too unhappy) to continue.

It's not a perfect answer but it's the best solution we've found so far.

Condition expectations

It's been a saying on my training programmes for some years that if a deal isn't earned then it won't be valued.

Concessions that are given too easily are often banked and then disregarded. If something is easy to give then there has to be plenty more to come. That's the value of a good flinch – it shows the pain of the concession.

One way round this is to set up a conditioning programme whereby if you're a seller you explain to a buyer that resources are finite and that you may not be able to satisfy them. You'll do your best but you can't make any promises no matter how valuable the business.

As a buyer you're talking about the incumbent supplier and how much you value them and how difficult it is to change suppliers.

Let the other party know that winning your business isn't something to be taken for granted. That way your concessions, when placed in this context, will have much more perceived value.

Manage perceptions

There are lots of definitions for negotiation. One, I know, talks about the division of scarce resources; another about moving a person from one opinion to another; yet another talks about obtaining objectives.

Definitions of commercial negotiation that I prefer always contain some reference towards moving towards a 'fair' agreement.

If an agreement is perceived to be unfair by one of the parties then the deal will have almost no future. The agreement will be resented and at the earliest opportunity the aggrieved party will seek to annul or sabotage the deal.

Fairness is, of course, a matter of opinion and cannot be measured. The effective negotiator is always looking to influence the other party to ensure that they perceive the deal as fair and reasonable. Fair deals last a long time and help to build better relationships. It's worth spending the time creating this perception.

Understand the basics of human nature

A great deal has been written about motivation and how you might be able to factor it in to a business deal.

You might think of Maslow's hierarchy of needs, Hertzberg's hygiene factors or Vroom's expectancy theory.

Here's something that's a whole lot simpler. Most people in business are motivated by just two things: fear and greed.

If you can ensure that the greed factor is well lubricated (benefits, advantages, cash flow improvements, bonus payments etc.) and the fear factor is well represented (loss of business, decline in market share, unhappy customers etc.) your deals will progress a whole lot more easily.

Sometimes human nature is not a pretty sight but nobody ever became poor underestimating human nature.

Show diplomacy

Right from the outset it must be stated that it is wrong to lie in a negotiation. People who lie destroy relationships and acting immorally is against the ethical code of most organisations.

Does this mean that you must always tell the truth? Very certainly not!

There is a very large area of activity between lying at one end of the continuum and always telling the truth at the other.

As children we are often taught not to be hurtful to our friends. When a friend asks, *"What do you think of my dress?"* it would be unkind to be brutally frank. We find a diplomatic way of putting our feelings forward. Is this a lie? Maybe.

When a supplier asks, *"So what do you think of my product?"* do you say, *"It's just fantastic, a world beater,"* (the truth) or maybe *"It fulfils all of our selection criteria along with a whole host of other short-listed products"* (also the truth).

When I tell a client that my diary is *"pretty full"* and that I might be able to squeeze them in, am I lying, exaggerating or telling the truth if I only have two days' work that week. *"Pretty full"* is certainly a matter of opinion (my opinion, that is).

I'd say that the hunt for the truth is a vain hunt. Don't tell lies, for sure, but then don't always tell the truth. How does that sound?

Just ask

There is a difference between selling and negotiating and often it's clearest at the end of the business meeting.

Sales people are often very reluctant to ask the close out question.

"Will you buy my product?" is a question no seller relishes because it gives the buyer the chance to say *"No"*.

On this basis sellers learn lots of closing techniques that help prevent this negative opportunity. Many of them are manipulative and are not designed to foster good long-term relationships.

Good negotiators shouldn't have to suffer in this manner. If you've scoped the deal well, prepared the ground, checked the situation and have been careful in leading towards a conclusion then all you need to do is ask.

"Do we have a deal, then?" shouldn't cause nightmares. The answer might be *"No"* but we know that we can't close every deal, every time.

Just ask, it's the simplest and most straightforward method of closing a deal.

Turn "No" into "Yes"

Negotiations always start with the word *"No"*.

They must really, if you think about it, because if there was a *"Yes"* then there'd be no reason to negotiate. It would mean that the other side and you had perfect harmony and that you had reached your goal and had no further journey to travel.

People negotiate when there's a problem to be resolved, when resources are scarce and especially when you've asked for something and the answer was a *"No"*.

My model suggests that when faced with a negative we use persuasive means to get the other person round on our side. Added to this, of course, is the fact that we want the other party on our side willingly and not with their arm twisted, which could hurt the relationship.

So...when you next hear the word *"No"* don't just shrug your shoulders and accept defeat. Negotiate and try persuasion until you hear the magic word, *"Yes"*. This will probably mean that you've established your objective.

(Unless of course your objective was so easy to achieve that it was just a formality to the other side. But you wouldn't be so lacking in ambition, would you?)

Stick to one point

Neil Rackham is one of the modern gurus of selling and negotiating and he suggests this technique as being a powerful help in a negotiation.

If the other party asks you what your objections are or what ideas you have you generally go straight in with your strongest and most powerful piece of logic.

If they then ask you what other issues are important or what other problems you have you'll probably move to your second point which is maybe not so strong as your first point. By the time you've reached your third or fourth point your statements could be sounding quite weak.

Rackham suggests that more arguments do not add value. In fact they dilute the effectiveness of your case.

Always put forward your strongest point first and if you're asked for other points just repeat your first point again and state that it is this point that needs to be resolved before you move on. Stick to one strong point rather than diluting it.

Collect things

Effective negotiators are by definition acquisitive people. They collect things during a negotiation and shouldn't have to give too much away in return.

One definition of negotiation is that it concerns the division of scarce resources and if that is the case then whatever the resource is that is scarce a good negotiator will want their fair (or maybe to some people even an unfair) share.

A delegate on one of my programmes once accused me of teaching people to be greedy. He believed that there was a fair share in a deal and to ask for more was greedy.

My problem with that is the apportionment of a fair amount. That's clearly a matter of opinion and some of the people opposite me in negotiations have had some very strange opinions of what is fair.

So...don't be embarrassed. If you want it, ask for it and go get it...You'll have to manage the consequences but that's the part that expert negotiators do so well.

Manage strategy and tactics

I've mentioned before that you can't fix a strategic problem with a tactical solution.

Let's see what we can do...

An effective negotiator has both a strategic plan and a tactical plan.

The strategic plan looks at the long-term relationship with the other party and essentially asks the question, *"Where do we want to be with these people over the long term and how does that fit in with our business needs and plans?"*

A tactical plan examines and plots the behaviours and ideas required when we meet the other party over the negotiation table. It is short term and based on how we can achieve advantage during the meeting itself.

So...have your long-term strategy organised and then fit your short-term tactics to help you achieve this.

That's a powerful combination and will give you a large competitive advantage.

Develop a portfolio

On my training programmes for more inexperienced negotiators I tell them that it is important not to limit their ambition and not to be the first person to put down a marker. This is a powerful learning point.

In contrast to this I teach on our more advanced programmes how best to put down a marker and when it might even be beneficial to go first.

These are not contradictory pieces of advice. The first refers to a low-value simple transactional negotiation and the second to a more complex relationship based piece of business.

Experienced negotiators need to have a portfolio of different styles and methods to suit each occasion. I have now developed a methodology for six different situations where very different principles and practices apply.

By all means learn the basics and apply them well but remember that as you progress through the business spectrum you will need to use very different tools, techniques and styles.

Balance the long and short term

Experienced negotiators ensure that they cover both the tactics of the negotiation and the strategy in their preparation.

The tactics lie within the meeting that they'll have. The behaviours, agenda, organisation and ebb and flow of the argument will all be covered and there should be no surprises.

Quite separately negotiators should be looking at the wider perspective and the longer timeframe. Market analysis will be important (Porter's five forces and PESTLE analysis will be used among other tools) and a long-term relationship management plan will be drawn up.

Negotiation continues to be a short-term quest for value (tactics) with a long-term balance of relationship management (strategy).

Get out of the trenches

I believe that compromise should rightly have a low position in the hierarchy of persuaders. It is essentially a weak way of settling an issue...the splitting of the difference.

We must, however, be careful that in our reluctance to compromise we don't indulge ourselves in trench warfare where we fight from our position against an opposition throwing grenades from their position.

Roger Fisher and William Ury make the point excellently in *Getting to Yes* where they discuss the need to work from a position of joint interests rather than entrenched positions.

If we see negotiation as a joint problem-solving exercise then working with the other party to reach a positive solution is a wholly admirable, value adding activity and should not be confused with 50/50 type compromises where value is split not enhanced.

Believe in ability

Negotiation guru Gerard Nierenberg uses the following example: ask a group of small children if they can paint and the answer will be an overwhelming *"Yes"*.

Ask a group of adults if they can paint and the answer will be entirely different. Many will have persuaded themselves that they do not have the talent or the aptitude to be able to paint.

Negotiation is similar. If you believe that you can't negotiate then you never will; you'll get bad results which will reinforce your belief. It's a self-fulfilling prophecy. You give up trying.

Good negotiators know that they will often get poor results and not do so well. The difference is that they always learn from their experiences and endeavour to improve month after month.

Learn the Greater Fool theory

An investor was recently suggesting that they were going to get 'free money' courtesy of a new internet share flotation despite paying way over the top.

They didn't get anything this time as the opening price for once stubbornly refused to make people rich.

Never be the 'greater fool'. Many deals work on the basis that no matter how foolish you are there will always be someone more foolish than you for you to sell them on to.

What happens when the 'greatest fool' buys the last share or the last apartment in a property boom? There's nobody to sell to!

Make sure it's not you.

Treat money personally

Employees in large organisations are very prone to thinking that a million dollars is a small sum of money. This makes them very vulnerable to the small trader who counts every cent.

I have encountered a finance director who called every deal under $100000 a 'minor purchase' and let his admin assistant do the business.

Think as if the money were your own and if you ever hear yourself saying that a contract or a deal is 'only' a certain sum of money think again and remember the Scots: *"Many a mickle makes a muckle"*!

4

Practical Examples
&
Good Stories

I always remember the true stories and practical situations that I've been involved in and I try to communicate the key learning points in the tips. I also write down things I've read and which seem to hit home with a good learning point.

Sometimes it's best practice...sometime it's very bad practice...sometimes very funny...sometimes downright tragic.

Recognise value

I visited my favourite tailor in Hong Kong recently on the first floor of a block in Nathan Road.

I negotiated vigorously with him for a while about a jacket and finally used a threat saying that there was a tailor on the ground floor of the same building who was much cheaper.

The tailor looked me straight in the eyes and said, *"What him…he's a half-price tailor!"*…and there the negotiation stopped with the firm understanding that he wasn't going to move on price.

I have now decided that I will never be a 'half-price' consultant.

Lessons from a tailor

So here I am again in Hong Kong negotiating on the price of a shirt. I'm being quoted HK$800 which is an outrageous sum of money...in my opinion.

The reply was from the tailor was that it was the high quality of the cotton that caused the high price and that was that. I asked for a swatch of cheaper material that would be a lower price and he got out a book of material that looked like leftover dish rags.

Job done!

Ladies and gentleman...I present to you the Russian Front tactic...perfectly executed.

More lessons from a tailor

Now it's my wife's turn to buy a jacket and she's negotiating with the same tailor.

I'm in one half of the shop with my jacket and she's in the other half.

When it's time to pay I'm clearly going to use the Building Block tactic so that I can leverage both jackets and the HK$800 shirt that I bought in the last tip.

However…the tailor tells me that the men's section has a different till from the women's section and that both departments account for their work differently and therefore there can be no volume discount.

This guy is good.

Know the right price

I was asked recently to help a friend with a price negotiation.

Their words to me were…*"How much off their asking price do you think we'll be able to get?"*

The question was well intended but came at the problem from the wrong direction. The real question should have been…*"What's a fair price for this?"*

If you allow the seller to set the parameters of the deal with their asking price you're playing right into their hands. You're allowing them to condition you that a certain price is fair and reasonable…i.e. their price.

If they're asking $500000 don't try to negotiate that down just because you want a discount. Better is to say to yourself, *"How much is the right price for us to pay?"* and if that price is $400000 start with that as your target rather than the other party's inflated price.

In manufacturing we'd tell a buyer to do some price engineering to calculate exactly what it should cost to make…not merely to rely on the other party's calculation. That's the way forward…what's the right price…rather than how much can we get off their price.

Aim high

I'm helping a friend with a house purchase and we're the potential buyers in a private sale.

The seller has had a survey done with a price of £250k as their opinion. I congratulate the seller on their optimism.

We've looked at the market and think that £175k is fair and we're going in at £150k with a first bid with £175k as our walk away.

My friend thinks that we've no chance given the high nature of the original survey but then the original survey was commissioned by the sellers and serves their purpose not ours.

We lose nothing by aiming high. This is a one-off negotiation where the relationship is nil. Every pound is an important pound and so I suggest we test the edges of this deal and see what their reaction is.

If they say *"No"* we've lost nothing...but it does condition them that we're not going to pay a very high price and that might be to our advantage on the second and third round of negotiations.

Take advantage of a good deal

I recently stayed in a hotel that was particularly attractive and the client had negotiated a strong corporate rate.

I asked the client if we could piggy back his rate and now we stay at that hotel ourselves at the original corporate rate.

This is a good example of win/win/win negotiation. We are getting a rate beyond what we could achieve with our small volume; the client is getting extra volume on their account so that they can leverage an even better deal next time; and the hotel is getting more business than it would have done otherwise plus the good publicity and extra drinks, meals etc.

The world is full of good deals. Some of them may not be yours but that does not mean that you shouldn't try to take advantage of them. It could add value beyond what you might have calculated for yourself alone and it can create good will.

It almost sounds like the negotiation equivalent of perpetual motion. It seems everyone's a winner in this example.

Know the value of customer networking

Time: 4.30pm
Date: 13 December 2003
Location: Los Angeles airport

I walk into a car rental office and give them the internet booking form.

They tell me that the car I ordered isn't available any more...end of line...but they can do me a Ford. It's a bit smaller but none the worse for that.

The good news is that for just $5 a day more they can give me a luxury model. I reluctantly accept having tried to bargain down the $5 amount. I need the space for the suitcases and don't want a small car.

Walk out to the parking lot. Lots of the original car I ordered all in a row. I've been lied to! Now do I go back and have an argument...well it's been a long flight and I want to get on with the journey. I swallow it.

So well done car hire company...great use of the Russian Front tactic. Present me with an unpleasant alternative (the Ford) and I pay more than I wanted.

Downside...one annoyed customer trying a new company next time...and over 2000 people in this network who now know about it.

Make good use of time

I received this note recently from a delegate on a training seminar. Here's what he wrote:

Recently at some high-level negotiations, principles and costs were at stake, and we had a major impasse. This was the only credible contractor and we thought that we were backed into a corner.

Therefore we took a 'timeout' and telephoned our lords and masters for guidance. There were lengthy deliberations during the timeout that took some time, almost an hour. But nobody could see a way forward. Failure! But where would we go, what do we do now?

Eventually we returned to the meeting room, to 'face the music', but before we could sit down the contractor started talking.

They relented on a number of key issues, without us speaking a word. We also remained stone faced and silent on our return to our seats.

It appeared that the contractor was also in the same difficult position and during the timeout they had reflected on the possibility of losing the contract, credibility issues etc. etc. It goes without saying that they believed that their loss was greater than ours...who knows?

Conclusion, another success story! With minimal effort and the unsuspecting/helping hand of the contractor.

Ringfence the profit

One of the aspects of supply chain management that comes up frequently in negotiations is the issue of profit and margin.

Buyers will calculate that the net margin of a product is 8% and that costs (in their various forms) come to 92%.

What we're now advising many buyers is that when it comes to negotiating the price it may be more effective to concentrate on the costs rather than the margin. Certainly a target of 92% is a better target to aim for than one of 8%.

A seller who sees a buyer constantly attacking their margin is never going to participate in a collaborative negotiation. If the buyer said, however, *"Let's ringfence the margin at 8% and see what we can do with the rest...."* they'd suddenly find a much more enthusiastic supplier who was prepared to share information and participate in the process.

A deal I was involved with recently concerned a raw material percentage of some 85% of total costs. It transpired that the buyer could obtain the material much cheaper than the supplier and therefore by a process of free issue of materials real cost savings were achieved that did not impinge on the supplier's margin.

Condition the seller

I was in a coin dealer's shop recently in New York when a man came in with a box of coins and asked the dealer if he could have a look and maybe make him an offer.

The dealer looked at the coins and one by one took them out. As each coin was placed on the counter it was accompanied by a shake of the head and a regret that it was 'only' whatever it was. Every coin was either too old, too young, too dirty, too clean…in fact the dealer couldn't find a good word to say about any of the coins.

The seller spent all this time shaking his head sadly being reconciled to his fate that his collection wasn't really worth as much as he thought. At the end of the process the dealer offered a derisory sum and the seller accepted it saying that it was a shame that the collection wasn't more valuable.

Maybe the dealer was acting perfectly honestly but nonetheless he did a really fine job of conditioning the seller that when the offer came it would be a low one.

Conditioning is a powerful technique. If we can get the other side conditioned to have low expectations before we have to put down a marker our job is already half done and most of the 'work' has been by our negotiation counterparts.

Behave like a hero

Emmanuel Lasker was the world chess champion at the beginning of the twentieth century. He was on a transatlantic voyage and one of the passengers asked him for a game of chess. When Lasker was hesitant the other passenger misjudged the reason and offered to concede Lasker a queen in the game if it would help him.

Lasker played the man and received a queen start and deliberately lost.

Lasker then said, *"I think it helped you to be without a Queen. Let's play another game and this time I will give you a queen."*

The man protested and probably thought that Lasker was crazy but Lasker insisted and duly trounced the man.

Lasker said, *"See, I told you having a queen was a disadvantage!"*

Later on the man found out who Lasker was and was more than a little embarrassed.

When you're really good you don't have to keep proving it with bullying tactics and use of power. It causes resentment. Sometimes a nice, self-deprecating move creates real respect in the other party rather than contempt.

When you're good or have seniority or power don't abuse it. It might only be temporary and people have very long memories.

Remain ready to pay for value

A couple of weeks ago I walked into a shop and asked a few questions about their products. The owner of the shop gave me personal service for 20 minutes even though they were busy. He showed me a range of products and made some well-focused suggestions on what I should buy.

In the end I parted with over $500 and left the shop happy.

I didn't negotiate and I readily paid the full asking price.

Questions:

Should I have negotiated?

Did I get value?

Did the shop owner expect me to negotiate?

Have I got more money than sense?

Was I just a happy shopper who thought that such good service should be rewarded?

Was I building a good relationship for next time?

You choose!

Negotiate on time

A friend tells me the story when he was recently part of a team looking at the procurement of some equipment.

There was a negotiation with the account manager then a further one with the account manager's boss.

Finally approval was needed from their CEO in the States.

So proud was the seller's boss that *"this was a never to be repeated deal better than any other company had ever achieved,"* that he stated that he had agreed with his CEO that he would announce the deal at the annual sales convention (later that week).

Accordingly the UK buyers delayed the confirmation and any communication to the evening before the conference. When the sales manager eventually got in touch he was more than a little worried. They then declined his offer suggesting a need to look at alternatives.

At that stage the concessions and added value flowed without any pushing. In the end the seller even thanked them. Job done.

Show readiness to negotiate

In my never-ending search for a nice handmade shirt I was in a Hong Kong tailor recently asking for prices. He quoted me HK$700 which is a truly outrageous sum but I was in a good mood and ready to make a purchase. I tried to talk about volume (2 shirts!) he merely doubled the price.

I then vainly tried to explain that it was expensive and that a discount was obviously in order when he uttered the fateful words: 'fixed price'. I checked that I had heard this correctly and he repeated the sentence.

I was out of the door like a shot. Nobody ever pays a fixed price in a tailor's in Hong Kong. It's a matter of pride.

Just imagine a different scenario. The tailor adds in the discount to the original price. I bargain hard and he gives me a discount and then I buy the shirt and we're all happy.

Being a firm negotiator is a powerful thing but you need to get the psychology right and not alienate the other party especially when they have money in their pocket.

Know when to pay full price

The Glaser company make high quality luggage and leather goods from their factory in San Francisco. On my first visit there I saw a briefcase and decided that I wished to buy it after planning to negotiate the very high price down considerably.

I explained my price predicament to the seller and awaited his reply. He looked me straight in the eyes and uttered the fateful words, *"You're right, Tom, it is a high price and many customers can't afford our bags."*

This was followed by silence and plenty more eye contact. This was the most friendly and disarming threat that I've ever received. The clear message was, *"Pay up or go,"* but put in such a charming way.

So...being a top international expert I duly paid up the full list price and walked out a happy (but considerably poorer) man.

Show ambition

I ran a class this week and suggested to one of the members that they might try to look for a 40% saving on budget.

Their comment was, *"How could that be possible? Nobody could give you that."*

Well, they were half right. If you think you can't get it then you won't ask and then you won't get it and then you won't be disappointed. It's a strange self-justifying circle.

Our records from all over the world suggest that a lack of ambition is more often than not the limiting factor in achieving great results.

Be credible, obviously, but be ambitious. I have a recorded saving of 48% off a current spend with one client.

You could do the same….if you're ambitious!

Question assumptions regularly

A farmer put up an electric fence around his pasture to keep the cows in. It worked perfectly. A year later his neighbour complimented him on his fence but regretted that he could not afford the electricity bill.

The first farmer laughed and said that he'd turned the power off after a week which was just long enough for each cow to get one shock and learn to keep away from the fence.

Make sure that you're not one of these cows. Have you been conditioned by the other side never to ask for something or do you genuinely believe that something could never happen?

If you really believe something can never happen then it never will! Question all of your assumptions regularly and don't get conditioned by the other side.

Use the power of emotion

Whilst on holiday to a Greek island a friend decided on an iced drink at a very Greek and isolated bar. The elderly owners treated him and his wife as long-lost friends. Having served the drinks the little old lady returned from her garden with a large spray of jasmine for my colleague's wife.

As they were about to leave the old lady reappeared with a very fine crocheted lace mat – cost £5. It was beautiful but expensive for the island.

My friend started to negotiate, only to be told by his wife not to be so mean, that the little old lady was a lovely person and that he shouldn't be so mean.

Never underestimate the power of emotion.

Use all the variables

I bought some print work this week and accepted the quote from the printer without asking for a cent off.

Why?...Because the printer put some effort into understanding my needs (relationship) and second because in this particular deal quality is far more important than price.

I can now feel a whole lot better giving him a hard time on the proofs and the bindings and the cover etc. than I could have done if he'd reduced the specification of the quote and given me a rock bottom price.

In many deals the buyers are not price sensitive and sellers should understand which variables are really important. The printer spent his time investing in the quality of the deal rather than shaving points off the price and that suited me just fine.

See other people's viewpoint

I've just spent a weekend away on a break learning more about a favourite hobby. It wasn't cheap but the consultant running the programme was experienced and good natured and the social facilities were excellent. All in all, I thought it represented great value.

Another member of the party didn't quite see it that way and thought the weekend expensive. His perception of value was different from mine.

So we learn…first that you can't please all the people all the time and second that people will pay extra and still be pleased if they can perceive real value.

Put yourself the other side's shoes and try to picture the value in the deal from their viewpoint.

Never rush a deal

When negotiating the price in a shop in New Zealand I was told that the prices would go up at midnight and that I should make up my mind quickly. I explained that I would have to think about it and would return the next day to continue the discussion.

It was my feeling that even if the prices did go up at midnight I could still get 'yesterday's' prices but all in all it looked as if it were a cheap tactic. This tactic is known as Standing Room Only and many negotiators rush into a deal because they think they'll miss the bus.

Pretty much without exception there's always another bus just a minute or two later.

Be thoughtful and don't rush into a deal. It's a long bus ride!

Search out the variables

I bought a radio this week. The price was non-negotiable...well, I couldn't get a discount!

The salesperson then asked me if I wanted some batteries. Of course I thanked him for his kindness.

Unfortunately it was not the offer of a gift but the offer of an opportunity to purchase. I declined.

I explained to the seller that I'd just bought an expensive radio (logic) and that surely he wasn't going to stiff me (said with a smile) for a set of batteries. Of course not. With a smile the batteries were added in free.

Sellers may not always be able to discount the price but they do have discretion elsewhere.

Search out the variables and add value to the deal.

See through the expert

I recently went into a car dealer's to get a new rear tyre. I said to the technician, *"I need a new tyre, please."* His reply as he looked at the front tyres was, *"Must be a couple for the front, then."*

When I explained that all I wanted was one single rear tyre, his reply was, *"Well if you say so, sir. You're the one taking the risk."* He then gave a great look that would have done credit to Robert de Niro.

In fact I knew well that the tyres were both safe and legal and had many miles left in them. Don't be threatened like this. It's clearly a tactic to make you buy stuff you don't need. Don't be persuaded by 'experts' into buying what you neither need nor want even if they are management consultants!

Check everything

Sonny Liston, the boxer, was discussing with Reg Gutteridge, the boxing commentator, the differences between blacks and whites. *"Black men have fewer hairs on their legs,"* said Liston. *"Not true,"* said Gutteridge.

They struck a £10 bet and Liston rolled up his trousers to reveal just two hairs on his shin. Undaunted Gutteridge rolled up his trousers to reveal a shiny false leg – the original was blown off during the Second World War.

Liston thought that hilarious and paid up.

Moral: believe nothing, check everything. Don't gamble unless you know all the facts and the odds.

Good news, bad news

I recently tried to buy a personalised number plate for my car via the internet. The advertised price was £1650, an outrageous amount for just a number...even if it was A1 TWB. Vanity is indeed a marvellous motivator.

Some days later I received an email entitled *"Good news about A1 TWB."* The message told me that the price of my number plate had gone UP by £100 and that the new price was £1750. What good news! It seemed that I was looking to buy a truly appreciating asset.

It was only a small logical connection to realise that if I got in quick now I could make even more money in the future. Time to get rich quick.

Even I didn't fall for that one. I wonder how much it's worth today! Did I really miss an opportunity?

Promote the power of logic

In a shoe shop this week I tried on a pair of shoes that had a scratch on the right shoe. The server then offered to sell some cream that would get rid of it.

I explained that at this price she should include the anti-scratch cream for free or give me a large discount or preferably both.

She said that she would use the cream herself and get rid of the scratch. She did this and the shoes came up perfectly.

She then asked if I'd like to buy this obviously very effective anti scratch-cream.

I smiled and declined. After all why should you need anti-scratch cream when your shoes don't have a scratch?

The power of logic wins again!

Never forget to ask for more

I was booking a hotel this week and decided to try to do it online. The price was £59 for one night.

I then went to the payment screen but the page was not working. I checked out the phone number and decided to call.

When I called, the person at the hotel offered me a rate of £49.95 for the night.

I was so pleased to 'save' nearly £10 that I booked immediately. In cold reflection I now realise how I had been conditioned by their website. The official rate of £59 was just a list price. Obviously if they could offer £49.95 over the telephone there must have been some more to give if only I'd asked. Heigh-ho...more money lost!

Perhaps I need to go on a training course!

Discount in small increments

I went into a shop recently in Hong Kong and saw an item that I wanted to buy. I asked for a discount and, lo and behold, I was offered a 50% reduction. It was jewellery!

Obviously I thanked them profusely, banked the money and went for more. Five minutes later another 5% was offered and accepted.

At that stage the discounts dried up and I had to decide whether to buy it at that discounted price. I felt a little uncertain because the 55% had been offered so quickly and the numbers didn't seem right.

You can't advise the shopkeeper when you're buying but if they'd discounted in smaller increments and made me work harder then I'd probably have paid more and been happier as well!

5

The International Perspective

I've taught in over 25 countries and always enjoy picking up a taste of each culture I'm in. I've read a great deal about this and I often share the best ideas.

When something good comes up I include it in the tips.

Never negotiate with strangers

There's nothing so simple as a good prejudice when it comes to dealing with people. It puts them in easily identifiable boxes and we can then say..."*We know what they're like...they're Germans*" (you can pick your own nationality).

This may be a good starting point in trying to get to know people better but it must never be the end point.

China is a good example. It has too diverse a culture to be able to put it all in one box. You have many languages and completely different ways of dealing with people. Within the Chinese 'family' we have: Shanghai, Hong Kong, Taipei and Singapore. All of them are 'Chinese' but are absolutely different.

I'm a Londoner and have little to do with the north of England...a sad benighted place full of meat pies, brass bands and whippets. I think you can get my drift.

Let's get to know people better...let's maybe start with some generalisations and even a geographic prejudice or two but let's then move on quickly to respect the individuals and their own personal situations.

If you want someone on your side you've got to get to know them. Don't negotiate with strangers and don't let your cultural prejudices get in the way.

Understand culture

When you meet people from different ethnic backgrounds you're often very aware that they all have different ways of doing things depending on where they come from.

I got involved with a negotiation in Hong Kong that involved Chinese, Japanese, Americans and a couple of Brits. About the only thing we could agree on at first was the day of the week.

Eventually we got there...when I asked the Hong Kong person on my team to get together with the other Chinese member of the other team and see if they could 'fix it' in Cantonese 'between us guys' as we were failing in the plenary session trying to do it all in English.

These international cultural differences are easy to spot and there's a great deal of literature on the subject. Trompenaars, Hofstede and Lewis are the 3 major gurus.

What's more interesting is when people from a similar culture have such different views of life. It may be courtesy of a corporate difference or just a personal view.

Don't wait until you see a foreign face before you think of being sensitive to cultural differences. The guy from nearby might be more 'foreign' than you think and it'll need all your sensitivity to work out a solution.

Understand cricket

I often joke with my American colleagues that the USA will never be a truly civilised place until they learn how to play cricket.

Here's why. A test match lasts five days...both sides bat twice and if at the end of it all there's no win then it's a draw and both sides go home happy. People can remember that some of the best test matches have been ones that ended in a draw.

Apart from the freaky tie from time to time all American sport ends up with a winner...and a loser. This idea of winning and losing is a powerful concept and coaches like Vince Lombardi have become famous explaining why.

If we take this into a negotiation we can often have a problem. Sometimes it's not easy to have a winner and a loser. Sometimes there's a genuine need to make concessions in order that the other side can progress. Sometimes we might like to take the long view... concede in the short term for long-term advantage.

Winning and losing are absolute concepts. They don't always sit well in a negotiation and analogies with sport are best chosen with care. Sometimes we need to be a bit more MCC and a bit less NBA.

See things as different

Within the Judeo-Christian tradition and culture we are very used to seeing a dialectic concerning what represents the appropriate path towards truth.

Too many cooks spoil the broth suggests that too much teamwork can be counter-productive and that some form of independence may be preferable.

BUT!

Two heads are better than one suggests that teamwork is also to be encouraged.

In a culture where this tension is common there is no jarring of advice. In other cultures where there are more shared values this would not have the same sense of reasonableness. The conflict of advice would not seem sensible or appropriate.

We can all see the glass as half full or half empty...this is a natural perception of a physical state.

Your challenge as a negotiator is to try to see life from the other person's viewpoint. Maybe they don't share your frame of reference in terms of what's reasonable. Don't be a cultural chauvinist and assume that your filter of the world must be correct.

Nothing much is ever right or wrong...just different.

Learn the ABC

It's never good practice to let the other party leave a negotiation feeling that they've not achieved anything. In Asian cultures the issue of giving face to the other party would always ensure that they had something to take away to show some form of 'success'.

This is a sound principle and we can achieve it simply by ensuring that we always ask for significantly more than we want.

Asking for more than we want allows the other party to beat you down to something more acceptable to them. That way they've had a clear 'success' and they can leave the table having achieved something valuable.

At the same time you may well have found that by aiming very high you've space to give the other party a real concession and still exceed your own original ambitions.

Obviously all of this comes within the strictures of our understanding of the radius of credibility. Aiming too high can damage your professional standing and leave the other party feeling uncertain about your real intentions.

Remember your ABC: ambitious but credible.

Pace the negotiation

Research done in artificial environments doesn't always transfer into a real negotiation room but in this case I think the theory is correct.

Research shows that the negotiator who is able to wait longer than the other party, to probe more patiently and appear less eager for a settlement will achieve a better result.

I teach that desperate people pay desperate prices and the converse must work also...that patient, ambitious people get more rewarding outcomes.

This is a well-known feature of many Asian negotiations, which take place at a slow pace and in which time can be a commodity of little importance.

Compare this to the average US negotiation and we have a clear point of departure. Time is a budget item in the USA and as such deals are done quicker and pursued with more vigour. This is fine when you're playing the home game but when the opposition come from a different background it helps to have a different style to apply.

Both parties should understand the value of both speeding up and slowing down when the need arises.

Know when to ask for help

I observed a negotiation recently between my clients, a Chinese company, and a Japanese supplier.

The negotiation took place in English as it provided a common platform.

My clients were not inconvenienced at all. Hong Kong managers can generally be expected to speak excellent English. Unfortunately the same could not be said of the Japanese suppliers who were at a clear disadvantage because of their lack of vocabulary and fluency.

What they required was a native speaker on their team who could have offered support in understanding some of the subtleties of the language.

My advice to all second-language negotiators is not to let pride get in the way of your asking a native-speaking colleague to sit in and help.

The payback could be enormous and the reduction in risk worth the effort alone.

Understand the other side

An international negotiation was so clearly constrained by local cultures that it seemed destined to fail. This was the spy plane problem between China and the USA.

George Bush clearly could not be seen to be weak. Weakness is not a popular commodity among US presidents (Jimmy Carter and Iran?) and being new he wasn't going to lose his first international test.

Jiang Zemin was another who couldn't be seen to lose personal face to another world leader especially given China's desire to be a world political and economic power (arms to Taiwan, entry to the WTO?).

Eventually a set of words was found whereby George Bush could say he never apologised and Jiang Zemin could clearly say he did.

So...understand American's love of winning and China's need for face and you'll do a whole lot better worldwide.

Never ignore the American way

More than 100 years ago Alexis de Tocqueville said of the American character: *"There is a tendency to abandon mature design to gratify a momentary passion."*

This is easily shown in the American desire to get down to business in a sharp and efficient way and to cut the deal with a minimum of fuss and time wasting.

Add to this the innate US love of winning and you have a potent cocktail of powerful and effective negotiation.

It may not be the only way nor indeed the best way but it certainly seems to be the American way. You ignore it at your peril.

Know the difference between 'big' and 'small'

Even though many international negotiations are conducted in English there is still a need to choose words carefully if you're playing an away game across cultures.

In the Western, American dominated culture, big is seen as powerful and negotiators will ask for 'large' discounts and 'significant' improvements. These are powerful words to their ears.

To the Eastern ear 'big' can often mean excessive and bloated and may even have a ring of discourtesy about it. In that culture 'small' is the way forward in asking for a substantial improvement.

Know your culture and choose your words carefully. It could lead to a big improvement (or is that a small improvement?).

6

The Power of Poker

I'm a keen poker player and have a library of books on poker every bit as large as my library of negotiation books.

I've found a great deal of crossover between the two activities and have written many tips on the subject.

Know the expected value

If you know anything about successful gambling you'll know that the concept of expected value (EV) is paramount.

Gamblers need to know what the EV is for their game and they usually calculate it per hour. If I'm a successful poker player then I need to know what my EV per hour. It's another expression for win rate.

When you negotiate you don't need to know your hourly win rate but you do need to know how much the deal is worth and what the size of the prize is. If you don't know exactly how many dollars are on the table and the cost and value of every concession given by you and the other party then you're negotiating in the dark.

As part of your planning ensure that you know exactly what value you're looking for…the cost of every concession given and gained…and what sort of success you are looking for.

If the financial parameters are fully defined you'll have no problem understanding what success looks like and whether you've achieved it.

Live to fight again

When you read a good book on gambling it directs you towards the four possible results of the gambling process:

> 1. You lose a lot.
> 2. You lose a little.
> 3. You win a lot.
> 4. You win little.

Successful gamblers always focus in on number 1. Never lose a lot...because that can be disastrous. Small losses can be endured and any sort of a win is better than a loss.

When you're negotiating start with outcome 1. Ask yourself the question: *"How can we avoid losing a lot... how can we avoid a disastrous outcome?"*

If all these major negatives are avoidable and you have a game plan to ensure this then you're left with just a small loss which is maybe allowable and any sort of profit which is bound to be good for business.

Don't be a gambler and put all your money on the high-risk option. Avoid big losses and live to fight another day.

Know the four options

In some respects poker is a simple game and we can learn from it.

Essentially with any hand there are only four betting decisions:

1. Fold...hopeless position...chuck it in.

2. Check...let's wait and see...reserve our position.

3. Bet...let's get some money on the table...promising position.

4. Raise...let's get some extra money on the table... excellent position.

So where's the analogy with negotiation?

If we need to fold in a negotiation then we'd better have a fire exit. We need to ensure that although the other party has a strong hand to play we're still in a position where we can survive. Survival is important.

We may be in a doubtful position…so let's play it cagey until we know better what they're holding. Check.

If we believe we're in a strong position then let's make some money…let's leverage the situation. But remember we want to play poker with these guys again next week so let's not steal all their money this week…or they won't be able to play next week.

Never hesitate

Let's play poker again…

If you're sitting opposite a player who is hesitating over his next move ask yourself *"Why?"*

People with good hands know what to do…they bet. People with bad hands aren't sure whether you're playing a bluff or if you've got a good hand…but because they've got a bad (or mediocre hand) they need to think what to do.

In a negotiation…if the other party calls a time out… ask yourself *"Why?"* Is it to celebrate their winning position or is it because they've got a tough dilemma and are not sure what to do?

Generally it's the latter. Weak players need time to think.

Of course the pros mix it up a bit…but that's why we play poker…and enjoy negotiations.

Cultivate a poker face

A man walks into a bar and sees a group of men playing poker at a table. Sitting with them is a dog.

The dog is holding the cards with his paws. The man's never seen anything like it before so he walks over to the table and says to the dog's owner:

"You must have a hell of a dog, there. I've never seen a dog playing poker before." The owner replies: *"It's no big deal really. The dog's not much good. Every time he picks up a good hand he wags his tail."*

So what's the lesson for negotiators...well, don't wag your tail. Don't show triumph because you got a better deal than you thought.

First of all you'll be giving away important strategic information to the other party and second you'll maybe create a great deal of resentment. People don't like to think they've been beaten.

People talk about a poker face...that's the answer. Don't let the other party know if you're desperate or elated. You'll do better in the long run...at poker and at negotiation.

THE POWER OF POKER

Never show machismo

So what happens when the irresistible force meets the immoveable object? The answer is that the immoveable object gets very badly jerked around.

Mike Caro, the poker guru, authored this comment and any garden variety matador knows this only too well.

When the bull is charging at you...don't just stand there to prove how brave you are...get out of the way!

In a negotiation...if you're dealing with a monopoly supplier or maybe your largest client there's little point in trying to prove your machismo by standing up to them and creating a showdown. If they have the irresistible force then show flexibility and try to go round them or under them. Going through them is not a worthwhile objective.

In New Zealand rugby they call it a Maori sidestep. It's rarely a winning negotiation tactic.

Count the money

At the end of a game of poker you only do one thing... you count the money.

At that stage you've only got three outcomes: more money, less money, same money. There's no winning or losing...just money to count.

Business negotiations should be more like this. Far too often people are determined to 'win' a negotiation irrespective of the cost in value terms.

So...at the end of a negotiation we need to have created value. That's pretty much the only reason we started to negotiate in the first place.

So...do you want to be a rich loser or a poor winner? If your desire is to be a poor winner then let me know who you are and I'll endeavour to negotiate with you more often. You can beat me up as much as you want and win and win...and I'll have all the cash.

Show me the money!

Play poker

Poker is a game that all negotiators should know about.

There are three elements to poker success:

Money management.

Understanding probability.

Understanding people.

Good poker players know how much cash to invest in a hand, how much cash they need to retain in order to survive. If the other side has more money than you then you're in a weak position irrespective of ability.

Poker is not a game of luck. The same people continue to win poker tournaments year after year. Good poker players know the odds...know when to bet...know when to fold. Poker is always a game of numbers.

Successful poker players can read people. They can sniff out a bluff when it's used on them. They know who the lions are and who the hyenas are. These are sensitive people skills. Negotiators need to do exactly the same... in equal proportion.

Practise the fundamentals

Here are some great words from David Sklansky, the guru of writers on poker:

"Being good at poker is something like being good at bowling or golf. You need talent to become a superstar no matter how much you know. However, with proper coaching, practice and study, most people should be able to achieve one notch below superstar status. Most people can become 190 bowlers or shoot 77 in golf if they have a coach who can show them all the fundamentals. It is not necessary that they have that much talent. With proper coaching, practice and study they can frequently surpass people who have much more talent but don't want to study and practise the fundamentals."

This is advice I have taken myself. My bookshelves are jammed with the best stuff written on negotiation (and poker!). I read with a highlighter in hand so that I can remember the key passages and try to put them into practice when I get the chance.

It really isn't difficult if you want to succeed.

Know the opposition from the start

One of the primary concerns of a poker player is the strength of the hands that the other players have.

Sometimes they advertise their holdings and it's easy to know what they hold. If they raise and raise then they're likely to have a strong hand.

Weak hands get thrown away.

Occasionally…tricky players mix up their plays so that it's not easy to guess their holding. This is the learning point for negotiators.

You know your hand (your position in the deal) but it's not easy to guess the position of the other party. Sometimes you'll be lucky and they'll actually tell you. Sometimes they act in a manner that gives their position away but sometimes they're tricky and you don't know if they're weak or strong.

This is where your homework and preparation come in. The more you know the other party the easier it will be to 'put them on a hand' and know exactly what their position is and their likely objectives and behaviours. Their previous behaviours will also give you a good picture of the business.

I often say that you can't negotiate well with strangers. It's tough to play poker with them as well.

Find out about local rules

A poker player walked into a club he hadn't visited before and started playing.

After a while he was dealt a monster hand (AAAKK) and duly bet it out with an expectation of a good win.

His opponent had 2-4-6-8-10 of red suits which is very weak.

He went to pick up the money but very quickly was told to look at the local rules which said that 2-4-6-8-10 of red suits was considered the best hand in this particular club. He lost his money.

He played on until one in the morning until he finally was dealt a 2-4-6-8-10 of red suits. He raised and raised and finally laid down his hand. His opponent had a pair of black 2s.

He went to pick up his money but was again told to look at the rules because after midnight black 2s are unbeatable. He lost again.

So what does this mean for a negotiator? You've got to know the local rules.

What are the T&Cs of this deal? How quickly will you get the cash and in what currency and at what exchange rate? What beartraps are there that you may not have spotted? Is there any legislation that may cause a problem?

Most of these will occur when you play away games. Working on foreign territory means that you must know all of the conditions of that territory.

You must do your homework and ensure that you know the rules before the hands are dealt.

Practice, practice, practice

I read a lot of books on poker and am always surprised at the crossover with the world of negotiation. Here's an example from poker pro, Lou Krieger.

Certain professions require taking action and making decisions under a great deal of pressure. Other professions require a great deal of considered logical thinking.

Research scientists are great thinkers but airline pilots may not have that luxury. When a warning light comes on they need to act quickly. It's a job that requires technical skill but not one for leisurely problem solving.

In an emergency they need to fall back on hundreds of hours of simulations where they've practised what to do if this particular situation were to occur. Computer simulations try to cover every conceivable problem that may occur and let the pilot learn the best and safest strategy.

Successful negotiators need time for substantial thought and planning but quite often decisions need to be taken quickly. Taking a recess every time a tough issue came up would not be an option.

You need to balance your experience and planning with an appreciation of the situation. One that you may have faced before and know the solution.

This can only be done by practice. If you're a negotiator and you don't practise ask yourself how you'll ever improve your performance and what you'll do next time a warning light comes on.

Have a clear plan

Everyone has choices to make in a negotiation. One of the key decisions will be the disclosure of information: how much, at what stage, in return for what etc.

It would be a fine world if both sides could trust each other enough to open their books and place their closest, most precious information on the table. Maybe that's a little optimistic.

It's certainly a tough world if both sides see a negotiation as a game of poker and keep their hands close to their chests.

Before you go into a negotiation you must decide very clearly what information you are prepared to divulge and what information you are protecting. It is not unacceptable to tell the other side that a piece of information is confidential.

Conversely you should have a list of the information that you require from the other side. They will then either give you this information or not. That's their decision.

Never let information slip out by mistake. Have a clear plan and keep to it.

Understand the process

There is a great deal of similarity between the world of poker and the world of negotiation. I was reading a poker book this week and it gave ten attributes for poker success. They were:

1. Be aware of your strengths and weaknesses.

2. Act responsibly.

3. Think.

4. Have a plan.

5. Set deadlines.

6. Be realistic.

7. Expect difficulties.

8. Build on small accomplishments.

9. Persist.

10. Have fun.

Seems like a pretty good way to negotiate.

Keep score

There's a saying in poker that you can't play for matchsticks, you've got to play for money and that's the only real way of keeping score. The person with the most money at the end is always the winner and generally the best player.

In poker you've got winners and losers and the real purpose of the game is to win all the other side's money. Relationships are unimportant...it's only the money that counts.

Negotiation isn't really like that. You'd find yourself a pretty unpopular and isolated person if all you ever saw were dollar signs hanging over every deal.

Let's remember that in negotiation we do care about the other side's feelings and we do want to build a relationship. The reason is that the other side probably has a whole lot of discretion to exercise and we'd rather like that discretion to be exercised in our favour.

It makes good business sense.

Bibliography

I've a huge library of negotiation books and they've helped me immensely with my weekly tips.

Credit must be given to the following people whose expertise far outweighs my own and whose ideas stimulated my thoughts:

Roger Fisher and William Ury: *Getting to Yes: Negotiating Agreement Without Giving In* (and authors of the BATNA principle)

Roger Dawson: *Secrets of Power Negotiating*

Danny Ertel and Roger Fisher: *Getting Ready to Negotiate: The Getting to Yes Workbook*

Neil Rackham: *Psychology of Negotiation* (audio tape)

Gerald Nierenberg: *The Art of Negotiating: How to Become a Skilled Negotiator* (Unabridged) (audio tape)

Michael Porter: *Competitive Strategy: Techniques for Analyzing Industries and Competitors*

Herb Cohen: *You can Negotiate Anything*

Join our e-mail newsletter

Gower is widely recognized as one of the world's leading publishers on management and business practice. Its programmes range from 1000-page handbooks through practical manuals to popular paperbacks. These cover all the main functions of management: human resource development, sales and marketing, project management, finance, etc. Gower also produces training videos and activities manuals on a wide range of management skills.

As our list is constantly developing you may find it difficult to keep abreast of new titles. With this in mind we offer a free e-mail news service, approximately once every two months, which provides a brief overview of the most recent titles and links into our catalogue, should you wish to read more or see sample pages.

To sign up to this service, send your request via e-mail to info@gowerpub.com. Please put your e-mail address in the body of the e-mail as confirmation of your agreement to receive information in this way.

GOWER